28/3/20

2

C

DØ755760

LEV

Please renew or return items by the date
shown on your receipt

www.hertsdirect.org/libraries

Renewals and
enquiries: 0300 123 4049

Textphone for hearing
or speech impaired   0300 123 4041

Hertfordshire

522 014 60 2

hamlyn | **all colour cookbook**

200 *Fast*
one pot meals

An Hachette UK Company

www.hachette.co.uk

First published in Great Britain in 2015 by Hamlyn
a division of Octopus Publishing Group Ltd, Endeavour
House, 189 Shaftesbury Avenue, London, WC2H 8JY
www.octopusbooks.co.uk

ISBN 13: 978-0-600-62905-4

A CIP catalogue record for this book is available
from the British Library.

Printed and bound in China

1 2 3 4 5 6 7 8 9 10

Both metric and imperial measurements have been given
in all recipes. Use one set of measurements only, and not a
mixture of both.

Standard level spoon measurements are used in all recipes.
1 tablespoon = 15 ml spoon
1 teaspoon = 5 ml spoon

Ovens should be preheated to the specified temperature
– if using a fan-assisted oven, follow the manufacturer's
instructions for adjusting the time and temperature.

Fresh herbs should be used unless otherwise stated.

Eggs should be medium unless otherwise stated. The
Department of Health advises that eggs should not be
consumed raw. This book contains dishes made with raw
or lightly cooked eggs. It is prudent for more vulnerable
people such as pregnant and nursing mothers, invalids, the
elderly, babies and young children to avoid uncooked or
lightly cooked dishes made with eggs. Once prepared these
dishes should be kept refrigerated and used promptly.

This book includes dishes made with nuts and nut
derivatives. It is advisable for customers with known allergic
reactions to nuts and nut derivatives and those who may be
potentially vulnerable to these allergies, such as pregnant
and nursing mothers, invalids, the elderly, babies and
children, to avoid dishes made with nuts and nut oils. It is
also prudent to check the labels of pre-prepared ingredients
for the possible inclusion of nut derivatives.

contents

introduction

This book offers a new and flexible approach to meal-planning for busy cooks and lets you choose the recipe option that best fits the time you have available. Inside you will find 200 dishes that will inspire you and motivate you to get cooking every day of the year.

All the recipes take a maximum of 30 minutes to cook. Some take as little as 20 minutes and, amazingly, many take only 10 minutes.

On every page you'll find a main recipe plus a short-cut version or a fancier variation if you have a bit more time to spare. Whatever you go for, you'll find a huge range of super-quick recipes to get you through the week.

one pot meals

With so many of us living busy lives these days, cooking dinner is enough of an effort without having to tackle a mountain of dishes afterwards. One pot dishes are simple to prepare – from an easy salad tossed together in a bowl, to quickly frying some meat and vegetables and then simmering in a flavourful liquid. All the recipes in this book require just one main cooking utensil, so once dinner is finished the clear-up is really easy.

choosing the right dish

Casserole dish: A heavy-based casserole dish is perfect for many one pot dishes

and there are plenty that are smart enough to bring from the hob to the table for a dinner party. They are best for making moist dishes like stews or curries. You can also find shallower casseroles that are great for cooking rice-based dishes. The best casseroles are made from cast iron, which is brilliant at retaining heat and ensuring even cooking. They can be pricy to buy, but they are an investment that should last you a lifetime.

Saucepan: Ideally, get a heavy-based pan so you can double up and use it for frying as well. A large pan will give you the space you need

to cook soup or pasta for the whole family, or any other recipe that requires a lot of liquid.

Frying pan: To ensure that food doesn't burn when cooking, look out for pans with a heavy base. Sticking is often a problem when frying, so try using a cast-iron pan and heating it until it is smoking hot – the heat will help prevent sticking – or you can use a nonstick pan. Sauté pans are deeper than frying pans, allowing you to fry more gently and making it easier to add a little stock or other liquid. You can also buy sauté pans with a lid, which allows you to steam food and keep it moist, or alternatively you can tightly cover the pan with tin foil. Frying pans have shallower sides and are best used when you really want to brown something over an intensive heat, like a steak.

Baking and roasting tins: Some of the simplest one pan dishes are cooked in the oven, so after a little prep work your job is done. A ceramic baking dish works well and many of these are elegant enough to bring to table. But a sturdy metal roasting tin is also useful. Try looking for versions with a handle, as this makes them easier to get out of the oven. To make sure your food gets browned in the oven, choose a tin that is shallow, otherwise the ingredients will simply steam.

Griddle pan: A griddle pan will bring the great taste of an outdoor barbecue to your kitchen. The metal dish can be heated on the hob and the ridges will give your food that special seared look. Cooking like this can be smoky, so it's worth having an extractor fan

a rounded bottom, but for electric or induction hobs, go for a wok with a flat bottom so it won't tip over during cooking.

using the best ingredients

Meat: Many one pot dishes use slower-cooking cuts taken from the shoulder or leg of the animal. These are tougher cuts and require a long and low simmering in the pot to produce tender meat. When time is of the essence you need to use quicker-cooking cuts such as loin. Taken from the middle of the animal, these cuts need to be cooked fast – if you leave them for a long time they toughen up and tend to dry out.

Ready-cooked vegetables: Ready-roasted vegetables are now widely available, and some grilled aubergine or courgettes will really lift a dish and save you lots of time and effort.

Canned pulses: Dried beans and pulses take time to cook from scratch, but are perfect for absorbing delicious flavours and filling you up. Luckily you can find most beans canned and they are simple to drain and rinse before using. You can find lentils in cans, but they are also available in microwavable pouches, which are quick to heat through.

Ready-cooked rice and noodles: You can now buy ready-cooked rice and noodles that are simple to make into a quick one

on. It's also a really healthy way to cook food. Don't add oil to the pan, rub a little oil over the surface of the food instead, then season and add to the pan.

Wok: You can cook large-portion meals in a wok, but make sure not to overcrowd the pan when stir-frying. Cut all the vegetables and meat to the same size so they cook quickly and evenly. Add items like noodles and rice at the end to get the maximum flavour. You can also use a wok for deep-fat frying, simmering and steaming, if it has a lid. Heavy woks are a good investment as they will ensure food doesn't burn, but nonstick versions are also available. For a gas flame, look for woks with pot supper. Cooked rice can be added or simply microwaved in the packet, while there is a large selection of noodles available to brighten up a stir-fry and couscous is the perfect quick-cooking ingredient.

Prepared pastry: Ready-made pastry is now widely available and you can also find ready-rolled pastry to make life easier still. Look out for pastry made with butter: it costs a little more, but the flavour is fantastic. In addition to puff and shortcrust pastry, try using filo pastry. These thin sheets, which crisp up in the oven, just need brushing over with melted butter or oil and can then be used to make savoury or sweet dishes.

the finishing touches

One pot dishes need to be packed full of flavour, so stock up on ingredients that will give your meals a sparkling finish such as herbs, spices and cheese. Using just one pot makes life in the kitchen much simpler, but it's easy to add side dishes without creating more stress. Bread is great with most meals. Choose a baguette to mop up a soupy stew, or in the warmer months, whip up a salad to enjoy with your meal.

poultry

lentil & chicken stew

Serves **4**

Total cooking time **10 minutes**

1 tablespoon **olive oil**

2 **chicken breasts**, each
    about 150 g (5 oz), thinly
    sliced

3 **celery sticks**, roughly
    chopped

4 **tomatoes**, roughly chopped

250 g (8 oz) **ready-cooked
    Puy lentils**

400 g (13 oz) can **chopped
    tomatoes**

1 **chicken stock cube**,
    crumbled

150 ml (¼ pint) **boiling water**

2 tablespoons chopped
    parsley

Heat the oil in a medium-sized, heavy-based frying pan and cook the chicken and celery for 5 minutes. Add the fresh tomatoes and stir for 1 minute.

Add the lentils, canned tomatoes and stock cube together with the measurement water. Bring to the boil and keep at a boil for 2 minutes, stirring occasionally.

Stir in the chopped parsley and serve ladled into serving bowls with crusty bread, if liked, to mop up the juices.

For thick red lentil & chicken stew, heat 1 tablespoon olive oil and cook 2 × 150 g (5 oz) thinly sliced chicken breasts, 1 large thinly sliced onion and 4 celery sticks over a moderately high heat for 5 minutes. Add 4 roughly chopped tomatoes, 250 g (8 oz) red lentils, 400 g (13 oz) can chopped tomatoes and 600 ml (1 pint) chicken stock. Bring to the boil, reduce the heat, cover and simmer, stirring occasionally, for 20 minutes or until the lentils are soft and tender. Season to taste and stir in 6 tablespoons chopped parsley. Serve with warm crusty bread. **Total cooking time 30 minutes.**

soy chicken with mushrooms

Serves **4**
Total cooking time **20 minutes**

4 small **skinless chicken
   breast fillets**
200 g (7 oz) **mixed
   mushrooms**
5 tablespoons **soy sauce**
finely grated rind and juice of
   ½ **lime**
1 **chilli**, sliced
1 **garlic clove**, chopped
1 teaspoon finely grated **fresh
   root ginger**
handful of chopped **fresh
   coriander**, to garnish
boiled **jasmine rice**, to serve
   (optional)

Set a large steamer over a saucepan of gently simmering water. Place the chicken and mushrooms in a shallow, heatproof dish that will fit inside the steamer. Mix together the remaining ingredients and spoon over the chicken.

Place the dish in the steamer, cover and cook for 15 minutes until the chicken is just cooked through. Scatter with coriander and serve with jasmine rice, if liked.

For soy-fried noodles with chicken & oyster mushrooms, heat a wok until smoking hot. Add 2 tablespoons vegetable oil and 300 g (10 oz) thinly sliced chicken breast. Stir-fry for 5 minutes, then add 1 crushed garlic clove, 1 teaspoon finely grated fresh root ginger and 200 g (7 oz) oyster mushrooms. Cook for a further 2 minutes. Stir in 300 g (10 oz) ready-cooked egg noodles, 100 g (3½ oz) baby spinach leaves and 4 tablespoons soy sauce mixed with 1 tablespoon sweet chilli sauce. Heat through until piping hot and serve immediately. **Total cooking time 10 minutes.**

chicken drumstick jambalaya

Serves **4**

Total cooking time **30 minutes**

1 tablespoon **sunflower oil**

8 **skinless chicken drumsticks**

1 **onion**, chopped

2 **garlic cloves**, crushed

2 **celery sticks**, sliced

1 **red chilli**, deseeded and chopped

1 **green pepper**, cored, deseeded and chopped

75 g (3 oz) **chorizo sausage**, sliced

250 ml (8 fl oz) **American long-grain rice**

500 ml (17 fl oz) **chicken stock**

1 **bay leaf**

3 **tomatoes**, cut into wedges

dash of **Tabasco sauce**

salt and **pepper**

Heat the oil in a large pan. Cut a few slashes across the thickest part of the drumsticks, add them to the pan and fry over a high heat for 5 minutes, turning occasionally. Add the onion, garlic, celery, chilli and pepper and cook for a further 2–3 minutes or until softened.

Add the chorizo, fry briefly, then add the rice, stirring to coat the grains in the pan juices. Pour in the stock, add the bay leaf and bring to the boil. Cover, reduce the heat and simmer for 20 minutes, stirring occasionally, until the stock has been absorbed and the rice is tender.

Stir in the tomatoes and Tabasco sauce and season to taste. Heat through for 3 minutes before serving.

For quick chicken & chorizo stew, pour 350 g (11½ oz) ready-made tomato and roasted pepper pasta sauce into a saucepan. Add 200 g (7 oz) chopped ready-cooked chicken, 75 g (3 oz) sliced chorizo and 400 g (13 oz) can butter beans, rinsed and drained. Simmer for 5 minutes and serve with crusty bread. **Total cooking time 10 minutes.**

thai red duck curry

Serves **4**
Total cooking time **30 minutes**

2 tablespoons **sunflower oil**
2 **garlic cloves**, crushed
1 teaspoon peeled and finely
   grated **fresh root ginger**
2 tablespoons **Thai red curry
   paste**
400 g (13 oz) **skinless duck
   breasts**, thinly sliced
400 ml (14 fl oz) **coconut milk**
200 g (7 oz) **mangetout**,
   halved lengthways
200 ml (7 fl oz) hot **chicken
   stock**
4 **kaffir lime leaves**
2 teaspoons grated **palm
   sugar** or **caster sugar**
2 **lemon grass stalks**, bruised
salt and **pepper**
handful of chopped **fresh
   coriander**, to garnish
steamed **jasmine rice**, to
   serve

Heat the oil in a large wok or frying pan until hot, add the garlic and ginger and stir-fry over a high heat for 20–30 seconds. Stir in the curry paste and stir-fry for 30 seconds, then add the duck and stir-fry for a further 4–5 minutes.

Stir in the coconut milk, mangetout, stock, lime leaves, sugar and lemon grass and bring to the boil, then reduce the heat to medium and cook, uncovered, for 15–20 minutes, stirring occasionally, until the duck is cooked through. Season to taste.

Ladle into bowls, scatter with chopped coriander and serve with steamed jasmine rice.

For Thai-style red duck salad, thinly slice 4 smoked duck breasts and put in a large salad bowl with a large handful of mixed salad leaves. Mix together 1 teaspoon Thai red curry paste, 6 tablespoons light olive oil, 2 teaspoons clear honey and 3 tablespoons red wine vinegar in a bowl, then season. Pour the dressing over the salad, toss to mix well and serve with warm crusty bread. **Total cooking time 10 minutes.**

french-style chicken stew

Serves **4**
Total cooking time **20 minutes**

1 **leek**, sliced

4 **boneless, skinless chicken thighs**, cut into chunks

400 g (13 oz) small **new potatoes**, halved

1 **carrot**, sliced

400 ml (14 fl oz) hot **chicken stock**

50 ml (2 fl oz) **dry white wine**

100 g (3½ oz) **frozen peas**, defrosted

2 tablespoons **crème fraîche**

salt and **pepper**

handful of chopped **tarragon**, to garnish

Place the leek, chicken, potatoes and carrot in a large saucepan. Pour in the stock and wine and season to taste.

Bring to the boil, then reduce the heat and simmer for 15 minutes until just cooked through.

Stir in the peas and crème fraîche and heat through. Scatter over the tarragon and serve immediately.

For chicken sauté with peas, lettuce & tarragon,

heat 1 tablespoon oil in a saucepan. Add 300 g (10 oz) thinly sliced chicken and cook for 2 minutes until golden. Add 1 crushed garlic clove and cook for a further 30 seconds. Pour in 25 ml (1 fl oz) dry white wine and bubble for 1 minute, then add 50 ml (2 fl oz) chicken stock and boil hard for 2 minutes. Stir in 100 g (3½ oz) defrosted frozen peas, 1 sliced Little Gem lettuce and 2 tablespoons crème fraîche, season to taste and heat through. Sprinkle with chopped tarragon and serve with lightly toasted baguette slices. **Total cooking time 10 minutes.**

chicken & sweetcorn chowder

Serves **4**
Total cooking time **10 minutes**

325 g (11 oz) can **creamed sweetcorn**
450 ml (¾ pint) **milk**
175 g (6 oz) **ready-cooked chicken**, torn into pieces
125 g (4 oz) **frozen sweetcorn kernels**
2 **spring onions**, chopped
2 teaspoons **cornflour**
salt and **pepper**
crusty bread, to serve

Place the creamed sweetcorn in a saucepan with the milk and heat, stirring.

Add the chicken, sweetcorn kernels and spring onions and season to taste. Simmer for 5 minutes, stirring occasionally.

Blend the cornflour with 1 tablespoon water, pour into the soup and stir to thicken. Ladle into bowls and serve with crusty bread.

For chicken, bacon & sweetcorn chowder, fry
2 chopped rashers of bacon with 1 chopped onion and 2 chopped medium potatoes in a knob of butter for 5 minutes. Pour in 500 ml (17 fl oz) milk and simmer for 10 minutes. Stir in 125 g (4 oz) frozen sweetcorn kernels and 175 g (6 oz) chopped ready-cooked chicken. Season to taste, heat through and serve sprinkled with chopped fresh parsley. **Total cooking time 20 minutes.**

turkey with pancetta & beans

Serves **4**

Total cooking time **30 minutes**

handful of chopped **rosemary**
handful of chopped **parsley**
25 g (1 oz) **butter**, softened
800 g (1¾ lb) **turkey breast
  joint**
6 **garlic cloves**
50 ml (2 fl oz) **dry white wine**
50 ml (2 fl oz) hot **chicken
  stock**
4 **pancetta slices**
2 x 400 g (13 oz) cans **butter
  beans**, rinsed and drained
handful of **sun-blush
  tomatoes**, roughly chopped
50 ml (2 fl oz) **double cream**
salt and **pepper**

Mix together the rosemary, three-quarters of the parsley and the butter and smear over the turkey joint. Season to taste.

Place in a roasting tin with the garlic cloves, pour the wine and stock into the tin and arrange the pancetta on top of the turkey. Place in a preheated oven, 220°C (425°F), Gas Mark 7, for 25 minutes.

Put the beans, tomatoes and cream into the roasting tin, topping up with a little water if necessary. Season to taste, then return to the oven for a further 3–5 minutes or until the turkey is cooked through and the beans are warm.

Cut the turkey into slices and arrange on plates with the crispy pancetta and the beans, sprinkled with the remaining parsley.

For turkey, bacon & bean stew, mix 400 g (13 oz) minced turkey with 2 finely chopped spring onions, 1 finely chopped bacon rasher and 1 egg yolk and season well. Roll the mixture into small balls. Heat 1 tablespoon oil in a deep frying pan. Fry the balls for 5 minutes until golden all over. Stir in 1 crushed garlic clove, then add a 200 g (7 oz) can chopped tomatoes and simmer for 5–10 minutes until the turkey balls are cooked through. Stir in a 400 g (13 oz) can butter beans, rinsed and drained, and heat through. Season to taste and scatter with parsley to serve. **Total cooking time 20 minutes.**

chicken & spinach stew

Serves **4**
Total cooking time **20 minutes**

625 g (1 ¼ lb) **skinless,
  boneless chicken thighs**,
  thinly sliced
2 teaspoons **ground cumin**
1 teaspoon **ground ginger**
2 tablespoons **olive oil**
1 tablespoon **tomato purée**
2 x 400 g (13 oz) cans **cherry
  tomatoes**
50 g (2 oz) **raisins**
250 g (8 oz) **ready-cooked
  Puy lentils**
1 teaspoon grated **lemon** rind
150 g (5 oz) **baby spinach**
salt and **pepper**
handful of chopped **parsley**,
  to garnish
steamed **couscous** or **rice**,
  to serve

Mix the chicken with the ground spices until well
coated. Heat the olive oil in a large saucepan or
flameproof casserole dish, then add the chicken
and cook for 2–3 minutes, until lightly browned.

Stir in the tomato purée, tomatoes, raisins, lentils
and lemon rind, season and simmer gently for about
12 minutes, until thickened slightly and the chicken
is cooked.

Add the spinach and stir until wilted. Ladle the stew
into bowls, then scatter with parsley and serve with
steamed couscous or rice.

For chicken & rice soup with lemon, heat
2 tablespoons oil in a large saucepan and cook
4 sliced spring onions and 2 chopped garlic cloves
over a medium heat for 2–3 minutes, to soften. Add
200 g (7 oz) thinly sliced, skinless chicken breast and
cook for 3–4 minutes, until lightly browned all over.
Add 150 g (5 oz) washed long-grain rice and stir to coat
in the oil. Pour 1.2 litres (2 pints) of good-quality, hot
chicken or vegetable stock into the pan, season to taste,
add a pinch of freshly grated nutmeg, then simmer for
about 15 minutes, until the rice is tender. Stir 150 g
(5 oz) mixture of chopped watercress and spinach
leaves into the soup and stir for 1–2 minutes, until the
leaves have wilted. Ladle into bowls and serve with
lemon wedges. **Total cooking time 30 minutes.**

spiced roast chicken with lime

Serves **4**
Total cooking time **30 minutes**

8 small **skinless chicken
   thighs**
1 tablespoon **harissa**
4 tablespoons **clear honey**
2 **limes**, cut into wedges
1 **red pepper**, cored,
   deseeded and cut into
   large chunks
2 **courgettes**, cut into chunks
1 **onion**, cut into wedges
300 g (10 oz) **new potatoes**,
   halved if large
1 tablespoon **olive oil**
salt and **pepper**

Cut a few slashes across each chicken thigh. Mix
together the harissa and honey and rub all over the
chicken thighs. Place in a roasting tin large enough to
spread everything out in a single layer, with the lime
wedges, red pepper, courgettes, onion and potatoes.

Drizzle over the oil, season and roast in a preheated
oven, 220°C (425°F), Gas Mark 7, for 25 minutes,
turning occasionally, or until the chicken is cooked and
the vegetables are tender. Serve with the juice of the
lime wedges squeezed over the chicken.

For pan-fried spicy chicken, cut 8 small skinless
chicken thigh fillets into strips and coat in a mixture
of 1 tablespoon harissa and 1 tablespoon clear honey.
Heat 1 tablespoon sunflower oil in a large frying
pan, add the chicken and fry over a medium heat for
5 minutes. Add 1 cored, deseeded and chopped red
pepper, 2 chopped courgettes, 1 onion, cut into thin
wedges, and 2 limes, cut into wedges. Cook for
10 minutes, stirring occasionally, or until the chicken
is cooked and the vegetables are tender. Serve with
new potatoes. **Total cooking time 20 minutes.**

mango & coconut curry

Serves **4**
Total cooking time **20 minutes**

1 tablespoon **vegetable oil**
1 large **onion**, chopped
500 g (1 lb) cubed **chicken meat**
1 large, ripe **mango**, peeled, stoned and cut into chunks
1 teaspoon **ground coriander**
1 teaspoon **ground cumin**
2 tablespoons **korma curry paste**
400 ml (14 fl oz) **coconut milk**
300 ml (½ pint) **chicken stock**
6 tablespoons chopped **fresh coriander**
1 tablespoon **cornflour**

To serve (optional)
steamed rice
poppadoms

Heat the oil in a large, heavy-based frying pan or wok and cook the onion and chicken over a high heat for 5 minutes or until golden and beginning to soften.

Add the chopped mango, spices and curry paste and stir for a few seconds before adding the coconut milk and stock. Bring to the boil, then reduce the heat and simmer, uncovered and stirring occasionally, for 10–12 minutes, then add the fresh coriander.

Blend the cornflour with 2 tablespoons water, pour into the hot curry and stir well to thicken. Serve with rice and poppadoms, if liked.

For pulpy mango & chicken curry, heat 1 tablespoon oil in a large, heavy-based frying pan and cook 375 g (12 oz) cubed chicken for 2 minutes. Add 2 tablespoons curry paste, 300 ml (½ pint) can mango pulp and 400 ml (14 fl oz) coconut milk. Bring to the boil, reduce the heat and simmer for 7 minutes. Add 250 g (8 oz) frozen peas for the final 3 minutes of cooking. Serve with toasted naan bread fingers. **Total cooking time 10 minutes.**

chicken & chorizo with lentils

Serves **2**
Total cooking time **10 minutes**

1 tablespoon **olive oil**
1 small **onion**, thinly sliced
125 g (4 oz) **chorizo sausage**,
   thinly sliced
300 g (10 oz) **skinless**
   chicken breast fillets, cubed
250 g (8 oz) pack **ready-**
   cooked green lentils
2 tablespoons **thyme leaves**
150 ml (¼ pint) hot **chicken**
   stock
1 tablespoon **Dijon mustard**
salt and **pepper**
crusty bread, to serve
   (optional)

Heat the oil in a large frying pan, add the onion, chorizo and chicken and cook over a medium-high heat for 5–7 minutes, stirring occasionally, until golden and the chicken is cooked through.

Add the lentils, thyme, stock and mustard and stir well to combine, then cook for a further 2 minutes until boiling. Season well with pepper and a little salt to taste. Serve with crusty bread, if liked.

For chicken, chorizo & lentil soup, heat 1 tablespoon olive oil in a large saucepan, add 1 roughly chopped onion, 125 g (4 oz) diced chorizo sausage and 150 g (5 oz) roughly cubed skinless chicken breast fillets and cook for 4–5 minutes until golden and the chicken is cooked through. Add 175 g (6 oz) green lentils and 500 ml (17 fl oz) hot chicken stock and bring to the boil. Reduce the heat, cover and simmer for 20 minutes until the lentils are tender. Stir in 1 tablespoon Dijon mustard and season well. Transfer the mixture to a food processor and whizz until almost smooth. Serve with crusty bread. **Total cooking time 30 minutes.**

chicken & tomato polenta pie

Serves **4**
Total cooking time **30 minutes**

2 tablespoons **olive oil**
300 g (10 oz) **skinless chicken breast fillets**, cubed
2 **garlic cloves**, finely chopped
1 teaspoon **tomato purée**
400 g (13 oz) can **chopped tomatoes**
pinch of **dried chilli flakes**
handful of chopped **basil**
1 **courgette**, sliced
500 g (1 lb) **ready-cooked polenta**, cut into 1 cm (½ inch) slices
25 g (1 oz) **Parmesan cheese**, grated
salt and **pepper**

Heat the oil in a shallow, flameproof casserole dish. Add the chicken, season to taste and cook for 3–4 minutes until starting to turn golden, then remove from the dish and set aside.

Add the garlic to the dish, cook for 1 minute, then add the tomato purée and tomatoes. Stir in the chilli and basil, bring to the boil, then reduce the heat and simmer for 10 minutes.

Return the chicken to the dish along with the courgette and cook for a further 5–10 minutes until the chicken is just cooked through.

Arrange the polenta slices on top of the chicken mixture, then scatter over the Parmesan. Cook under a preheated hot grill for 5 minutes or until golden and bubbling.

For sweetcorn, tomato & chicken salad, heat 1 tablespoon olive oil in a frying pan. Add 75 g (3 oz) fresh or canned sweetcorn kernels and cook for 3 minutes until browned. Chop 1 Cos lettuce and toss with 2 chopped tomatoes and 2 ready-cooked chicken breasts, torn into shreds. Mix 50 ml (2 fl oz) buttermilk with 1 teaspoon cider vinegar and 1 teaspoon sugar and season to taste. Scatter the sweetcorn over the salad, then drizzle over the buttermilk dressing and serve immediately. **Total cooking time 10 minutes.**

duck & figs with watercress salad

Serves **4**
Total cooking time **20 minutes**

4 **duck breast fillets**
4 **figs**, halved
½ teaspoon **ground cinnamon**
1 tablespoon **balsamic vinegar**
1 teaspoon **clear honey**
finely grated rind and juice of ½ **orange**
100 g (3½ oz) **watercress**
1 **chicory head**, leaves separated
salt and **pepper**

Use a sharp knife to score a criss-cross pattern on the skin of the duck and season to taste. Heat a large frying pan until hot, add the duck, skin side down, and cook for 7 minutes. Pour away the excess oil and turn the duck over. Arrange the figs in the pan and cook for a further 5–7 minutes until the duck is cooked through and the figs softened.

Remove the duck from the pan and cut into thick slices. Tip away any excess fat, then add the cinnamon, vinegar, honey and orange rind and juice to the pan and swirl around.

Divide the watercress and chicory between plates, place the figs and sliced duck on top, then spoon over the warm dressing and serve immediately.

For smoked duck, orange & fig salad, cut 4 figs in half, drizzle with a little olive oil and 1 teaspoon balsamic vinegar, then cook under a preheated hot grill for 2 minutes on each side until lightly charred. Toss 150 g (5 oz) watercress with 1 tablespoon sherry vinegar and 3 tablespoons olive oil and divide between serving plates. Peel 1 orange and cut into segments, then arrange on the plates with the grilled figs and 100 g (3½ oz) ready-made sliced smoked duck breast. **Total cooking time 10 minutes.**

greek chicken stifado

Serves **2**
Total cooking time **30 minutes**

3 tablespoons **olive oil**

2 **chicken quarters**

2 **shallots**, peeled and cut
in half

1 **fennel bulb**, trimmed and
cut into slim wedges

400 g (13 oz) can **artichokes**,
drained and halved

50 g (2 oz) **kalamata olives**,
pitted

3 tablespoons **sun-dried
tomato paste**

2 **tomatoes**, roughly chopped

1 tablespoon **rosemary
leaves**

300 ml (½ pint) hot **chicken
stock**

warm **crusty bread**, to serve
(optional)

Heat the oil in a large frying pan, add the chicken, skin side down, shallots and fennel wedges and cook over a medium-high heat for 10 minutes until the chicken is golden.

Turn the chicken over and add the artichokes, olives, tomato paste, tomatoes, rosemary and stock and stir well, then cover tightly and simmer for 15–20 minutes until the chicken is cooked through and the tomatoes have softened, adding a little water if the sauce is too thick. Serve with warm crusty bread to mop up the juices, if liked.

For chicken, artichoke & olive pan-fry, heat 2 tablespoons olive oil in a large frying pan, add 300 g (10 oz) thinly sliced skinless chicken breast fillets and cook over a high heat until golden, then add 1 teaspoon rosemary leaves, a 400 g (13 oz) can artichokes, drained and halved, 75 g (3 oz) pitted black olives and a 300 g (10 oz) jar tomato pasta sauce with vegetables and cook for 5 minutes until piping hot and the chicken is cooked through. Serve with ready-cooked rice or warm crusty bread to mop up the juices. **Total cooking time 10 minutes.**

jerk chicken & sweet potato soup

Serves **4–6**
Total cooking time **20 minutes**

2 tablespoons **vegetable oil**
1 **red onion**, chopped
1 **celery stick**, chopped
2.5 cm (1 inch) piece of **fresh root ginger**, peeled and chopped
1 tablespoon **jerk seasoning**
1 kg (2 lb) **sweet potato**, chopped (or use a mixture of sweet potato and butternut squash)
1.2 litres (2 pints) hot **chicken stock**
2 tablespoons **lime juice**
250 g (8 oz) **ready-cooked chicken**, shredded
salt and **pepper**
thinly sliced **spring onions**, to garnish

Heat the vegetable oil in a large pan and fry the onion, celery and ginger for 4–5 minutes, until beginning to soften. Add the jerk seasoning, then mix in the sweet potato and stir over the heat for 1 minute.

Pour the chicken stock into the pan and simmer over a medium heat for about 12 minutes, until the potato is tender. Blend to the desired consistency, then stir in the lime juice and season to taste.

Ladle the soup into bowls and top each with a handful of the shredded chicken. Garnish with spring onions and serve.

For quick jerk chicken broth, heat 2 tablespoons vegetable oil in a large saucepan over a medium heat and add 3 sliced spring onions and 1 tablespoon peeled and grated fresh root ginger. Cook for 1–2 minutes until softened. Stir in 1 tablespoon jerk seasoning and cook for 1 minute before pouring in 1.2 litres (2 pints) hot chicken stock. Simmer for 3–4 minutes, then take off the heat and stir in 250 g (8 oz) shredded ready-cooked chicken and 1–2 tablespoons lime juice. Ladle into bowls and serve, garnished with extra sliced spring onions, if liked. **Total cooking time 10 minutes.**

chicken with lemon & olives

Serves **4**
Total cooking time **30 minutes**

pinch of **saffron threads**
4 **chicken drumsticks** and
  4 small **chicken thighs**,
  skinned
1 **lemon**, halved
2 tablespoon **clear honey**
150 ml (¼ pint) **dry white
  wine**
125 g (4 oz) **green olives**
salt and **pepper**
2 tablespoons roughly
  chopped **flat leaf parsley**,
  to garnish

To serve (optional)
new potatoes
green beans

Soak the saffron in 1 tablespoon boiling water. Cut
a couple of slashes across the top of each piece of
chicken and season. Spread out the chicken in a large
roasting tin or ovenproof dish and squeeze over the
lemon halves.

Drizzle over the honey, pour over the saffron threads
and soaking water and add the white wine. Roast in
a preheated oven, 220°C (425°F), Gas Mark 7, for
20 minutes, basting with the juices occasionally. Add
the olives and cook for a further 5 minutes until the
chicken is cooked.

Sprinkle with parsley and serve with new potatoes
and green beans, if liked.

For lemon chicken stir-fry, heat 1 tablespoon
sunflower oil in a wok or large frying pan, add 410 g
(13½ oz) chicken mini-fillets and stir-fry over a high
heat for 5 minutes. Add 1 tablespoon clear honey,
4 tablespoons lemon juice, 4 tablespoons dry white
wine and 125 g (4 oz) green olives. Heat through for
2 minutes, season and serve with ready-made couscous
salad. **Total cooking time 10 minutes.**

chicken & boston beans

Serves **4**
Total cooking time **10 minutes**

1 tablespoon **olive oil**
2 **chicken breasts**, each about
   150 g (5 oz), thinly sliced
1 **onion**, thinly sliced
1 tablespoon **black treacle**
1 tablespoon **wholegrain**
   mustard
1 tablespoon **soft dark brown**
   sugar
400 g (13 oz) can **chopped**
   tomatoes
400 g (13 oz) can **baked**
   beans
3 tablespoons chopped
   parsley
pepper
4 thick slices **wholemeal**
   toast, to serve

Heat the oil in a medium-sized, heavy-based saucepan and cook the chicken and onion over a moderate heat for 3–4 minutes.

Add the treacle, mustard, sugar and tomatoes, bring to the boil and simmer for 2 minutes before adding the beans, then stir in the parsley and heat through for 1 minute.

Spoon the mixture on to the slices of wholemeal toast, season with pepper and serve immediately.

For paprika Boston baked beans with chicken & bacon, heat 2 tablespoons olive oil in a large frying pan and cook 1 thinly sliced onion, 2 thinly sliced chicken breasts and 4 rashers of chopped streaky bacon for 5 minutes or until golden, soft and cooked through. Add 1 teaspoon paprika, 1 tablespoon treacle, 1 tablespoon wholegrain mustard and 2 tablespoons soft dark brown sugar and stir well. Stir in 400 g (13 oz) can chopped tomatoes and 2 x 400 g (13 oz) cans cannellini beans, rinsed and drained. Bring to the boil, cover and simmer for 10 minutes, removing the lid for the final 2 minutes. Stir through 2 tablespoons chopped parsley and serve. Total cooking time 20 minutes.

chicken with cashews

Serves **2**

Total cooking time **10 minutes**

50 g (2 oz) **unsalted cashew nuts**

1 teaspoon **sesame oil**

2 **skinless chicken breast fillets**, cut into strips

1 **garlic clove**, crushed

1 cm (½ inch) piece **fresh root ginger**, grated

125 g (4 oz) **oyster mushrooms**, sliced

4 **spring onions**, thickly sliced diagonally

125 g (4 oz) **frozen soya beans**

6 tablespoons **oyster sauce**

Heat a wok or large frying pan until hot, add the cashew nuts and cook, stirring, for 1 minute or until golden, taking care not to let them burn. Tip them out of the pan on to a plate and set aside.

Place the oil in the pan along with the chicken strips and cook, stirring, for 3 minutes or until browned and cooked through.

Add the garlic, ginger, mushrooms and spring onions and cook for 2 minutes or until the mushrooms and onions are just tender. Add the soya beans and oyster sauce, bring to the boil and simmer for 2 minutes, adding a little water if the mixture is too dry. Sprinkle over the toasted cashew nuts before serving.

For ginger chicken & rice stir-fry, cook 2 chopped skinless chicken breast fillets in a large frying pan with 1 teaspoon sunflower oil, 1 teaspoon garlic paste, 1 teaspoon ginger paste, 4 sliced spring onions and 125 g (4 oz) frozen soya beans. Add 250 g (8 oz) ready-cooked egg-fried rice and a dash of sweet chilli sauce and soy sauce. Stir-fry until hot. **Total cooking time 10 minutes.**

paprika chicken with peppers

Serves **4**
Total cooking time **10 minutes**

1 tablespoon **sunflower oil**
400 g (13 oz) **chicken mini-
fillets**
1 teaspoon **garlic paste**
1 tablespoon **paprika**
175 g (6 oz) **frozen sliced
mixed peppers**
1 tablespoon **tomato purée**
150 ml (¼ pint) **soured cream**
salt and **pepper**
tagliatelle, to serve

Heat the oil in a large frying pan, add the chicken and stir-fry over a high heat for 5 minutes. Add the garlic paste, paprika, peppers and tomato purée and cook, stirring, for 3 minutes.

Stir in the soured cream, season to taste and heat through. Serve with tagliatelle.

For paprika chicken casserole, fry 4 skinless chicken breast fillets in 1 tablespoon sunflower oil for 5 minutes, turning once, until golden. Add 1 chopped onion and 1 cored, deseeded and chopped green pepper, fry for 3 minutes then stir in 1 tablespoon paprika, 1 tablespoon tomato purée and 400 g (13 oz) can chopped tomatoes. Simmer for 15 minutes, season to taste and stir in 150 ml (¼ pint) soured cream. Serve with mashed potato. **Total cooking time 30 minutes.**

turkey tikka skewers

Serves **4**
Total cooking time **20 minutes**

3 tablespoons **tikka masala curry paste**
2 tablespoons **natural yogurt**
500 g (1 lb) **cubed turkey breast**
1 large **onion**, cut into bite-sized pieces
1 large **green pepper**, cored, deseeded and cut into bite-sized pieces

To serve (optional)
basmati or **long-grain rice**
mango chutney

Mix the curry paste with the yogurt in a bowl, then add the cubed turkey. Mix well to coat, then thread onto 4–8 metal or pre-soaked wooden skewers with the chunks of onion and pepper. Arrange on the rack of a foil-lined grill tray.

Cook under a preheated medium grill for 12–15 minutes, turning occasionally, until thoroughly cooked and lightly charred.

Serve hot with basmati or long-grain rice and mango chutney, if liked.

For turkey tikka masala, heat 2 tablespoons vegetable oil in a large saucepan and cook 1 large roughly chopped onion and 1 cored, deseeded and diced green or red pepper for 7–8 minutes until softened. Stir 4 tablespoons tikka masala curry paste into the pan followed by 400 g (13 oz) cubed turkey breast. Stir to combine and seal the turkey, then add a 400 g (13 oz) can chopped tomatoes and 300 ml (½ pint) water. Bring to the boil, then reduce the heat and simmer gently, uncovered, for 12–15 minutes until the turkey is thoroughly cooked and the sauce has thickened. Stir 125 g (4 oz) full-fat natural yogurt into the curry before serving with basmati or long-grain rice. **Total cooking time 30 minutes.**

chicken with warm lentils & kale

Serves **4**
Total cooking time **20 minutes**

2 tablespoons **olive oil**
4 **skinless chicken breast fillets**
1 **garlic clove**, sliced
100 g (3½ oz) **kale**, chopped
250 g (8 oz) can **Puy lentils**, rinsed and drained
2 tablespoons **lemon juice**
75 g (3 oz) **sun-blush tomatoes**
75 g (3 oz) **soft goats' cheese**, crumbled
salt and **pepper**

Heat half the oil in a large frying pan. Add the chicken, season to taste and cook for 5 minutes, then turn over and cook for 2 minutes until golden all over.

Add the remaining oil to the pan along with the garlic, kale and a splash of water. Cover and cook for 7 minutes until the kale is tender and the chicken cooked through.

Stir in the lentils and heat through, then add the lemon juice and tomatoes. Check and adjust the seasoning if necessary.

Cut the chicken into thick slices and arrange on plates with the lentils. Scatter over the goats' cheese and serve immediately.

For hearty lentil, kale & chicken soup, heat 2 tablespoons olive oil in a saucepan. Add 1 finely chopped onion and cook gently for 5 minutes, then add 2 chopped garlic cloves, 1 teaspoon tomato purée and a pinch of dried chilli flakes and cook for a further 1 minute. Pour in 1.8 litres (3 pints) chicken stock and bring to the boil. Add 150 g (5 oz) dried red lentils and simmer for 5 minutes. Skim off any scum that rises to the surface, add 200 g (7 oz) cubed chicken breast and cook for a further 5 minutes. Add 100 g (3½ oz) chopped kale and simmer for 7 minutes until tender. Season to taste and serve in bowls with crusty bread. **Total cooking time 30 minutes.**

chicken, mushroom & dill pie

Serves **4**
Total cooking time **30 minutes**

1 tablespoon **vegetable oil**
1 **onion**, finely chopped
300 g (10 oz) **skinless chicken breast fillets**, cubed
150 g (5 oz) **mushrooms**, halved if large
3 tablespoons **dry white wine**
5 tablespoons **crème fraîche**
finely grated rind of 1 **lemon**
handful of chopped **dill**
3 large **filo pastry sheets**
40 g (1½ oz) **butter**, melted
salt and **pepper**

Heat the oil in a shallow, ovenproof casserole dish. Add the onion and cook for 2 minutes, then stir in the chicken and cook for a further 5 minutes. Add the mushrooms and continue to cook for 1 minute until starting to soften.

Pour in the wine, cook until it has bubbled away, then stir in the crème fraîche, lemon rind and dill and remove from the heat. Season to taste.

Meanwhile, unwrap the filo pastry and cover with a piece of damp kitchen paper until ready to use it. Working quickly, brush 1 sheet with melted butter and cut into 3 long strips. Arrange the strips on top of the chicken, scrunching it up a little. Repeat with the remaining pastry until the chicken is covered.

Brush all over with any remaining butter, then place in a preheated oven, 200°C (400°F), Gas Mark 6, for 15–20 minutes until the filo pastry is crisp and the chicken is cooked through.

For chicken & wild mushrooms in a creamy dill sauce, heat 1 tablespoon olive oil in a frying pan. Add 1 sliced onion and cook for 5 minutes until softened. Stir in 1 crushed garlic clove and 150 g (5 oz) mixed wild mushrooms. Cook for 3 minutes, then add 2 ready-cooked chicken breasts, torn into shreds, 3 tablespoons crème fraîche and 2 tablespoons chicken stock. Heat through, then add a handful of chopped dill and a good squeeze of lemon juice. Serve with garlic bread. **Total cooking time 10 minutes.**

chicken with mascarpone

Serves **4**

Total cooking time **20 minutes**

4 tablespoons **mascarpone cheese**

4 teaspoons **ready-made fresh green pesto**

4 **skinless chicken breast fillets**

3 tablespoons **olive oil**

100 g (3½ oz) **dried breadcrumbs**

150 g (5 oz) **cherry tomatoes**

25 g (1 oz) **toasted pine nuts**

salt and **pepper**

crusty bread, to serve (optional)

Mix together the mascarpone and pesto. Use a small, sharp knife to make a horizontal slit in the side of each chicken breast to form a pocket. Fill the pockets with the mascarpone mixture.

Season the chicken and rub with 1 tablespoon of the oil then turn in the breadcrumbs until well coated. Place in a baking tray, drizzle over another tablespoon of oil and cook in a preheated oven, 200°C (400°F), Gas Mark 6, for 10 minutes.

Add the tomatoes to the baking tray, season and drizzle with the remaining oil. Return to the oven for a further 5 minutes or until the chicken is cooked through. Scatter over the pine nuts and serve with crusty bread, if liked.

For chicken pizza melts with cheese & tomatoes,

cut 2 skinless chicken breast fillets in half horizontally and place on a lightly greased baking sheet. Top each with a slice of tomato and a slice of mozzarella cheese, then season to taste. Cook under a preheated hot grill for 7 minutes or until the cheese has melted and the chicken is cooked through. Serve in burger buns with a few salad leaves. **Total cooking time 10 minutes.**

chicken ratatouille

Serves **4**
Total cooking time **30 minutes**

8 small **skinless chicken thighs**
1 tablespoon **olive oil**
1 **onion**, chopped
1 **aubergine**, cut into bite-sized chunks
1 **green pepper**, cored, deseeded and cut into bite-sized chunks
1 **red pepper**, cored, deseeded and cut into bite-sized chunks
2 **courgettes**, chopped
1 **garlic clove**, crushed
400 g (13 oz) can **chopped tomatoes**
pinch of **caster sugar**
handful of **basil**, roughly torn
salt and **pepper**

Cut a couple of slashes across each chicken thigh and season. Heat the oil in a large deep frying pan, add the chicken and cook over a high heat for 5 minutes, turning occasionally.

Add the onion, aubergine, peppers, courgettes and garlic and cook for 10 minutes or until softened, adding a little water if the mixture becomes too dry.

Pour in the tomatoes, add the sugar, season to taste and bring to the boil, stirring. Reduce the heat, cover and simmer for 15 minutes, stirring occasionally. Stir in the basil and serve.

For chicken ratatouille with lentils, chop 4 boneless, skinless chicken breasts and fry in 1 tablespoon olive oil for 5 minutes. Add 1 chopped aubergine, 2 chopped courgettes, 2 drained and chopped roasted red peppers from a jar, 400 g (13 oz) can chopped tomatoes with garlic and herbs and 400 g (13 oz) can green lentils, rinsed and drained. Bring to the boil, reduce the heat, cover and simmer for 10 minutes. Sprinkle with chopped basil before serving. **Total cooking time 20 minutes.**

meat

tray-baked sausages with apples

Serves **4**

Total cooking time **30 minutes**

3 **red onions**, cut into wedges

3 **red apples**, cored and cut
into 6 wedges

200 g (7 oz) **baby carrots**,
scrubbed

3 **potatoes**, peeled and cut
into small cubes

4 tablespoons **olive oil**

12 good-quality **pork
sausages**

2 tablespoons chopped **sage
leaves**

1 tablespoon **rosemary
leaves**

3 tablespoons **clear honey**

salt and **pepper**

Scatter the wedges of onion and apple in a large,
shallow roasting tin with the carrots and potatoes.
Drizzle over the oil, then toss well to lightly coat all the
vegetables in the oil. Season generously. Arrange the
sausages in and around the vegetables, sprinkle over
the herbs and toss again.

Place in a preheated oven, 200°C (400°F), Gas Mark 6,
for 20–22 minutes until golden and cooked through.

Remove from the oven and drizzle over the honey. Toss
all the vegetables and sausages in the honey and serve.

For quick pork, apple & onion stir-fry, cut 250 g (8 oz)
pork fillet into very thin slices. Heat 2 tablespoons olive
oil in a large wok or heavy-based frying pan and stir-fry
the pork over a high heat for 2–3 minutes. Add 2 cored
apples and 2 red onions, each cut into slim wedges, and
stir-fry for 3–4 minutes until browned and softened.
Add 1 tablespoon chopped sage leaves or rosemary
and toss to mix. Serve in warm ciabatta with plenty
of Dijon mustard. **Total cooking time 10 minutes.**

italian beans with pancetta

Serves **4**
Total cooking time **10 minutes**

3 tablespoons **extra virgin
    olive oil**, plus extra to drizzle
300 g (10 oz) **cubed pancetta**
3 **banana shallots**, chopped
2 teaspoons chopped **thyme**
2 x 400 g (13 oz) cans **borlotti
    beans**, rinsed and drained
400 g (13 oz) can **cannellini
    beans**, rinsed and drained
200 ml (7 fl oz) **vegetable
    stock**
salt and **pepper**

To serve
crusty bread
Parmesan cheese, grated
chopped **parsley**

Heat the oil in a heavy-based frying pan and fry the
pancetta over a high heat for 2–3 minutes, until golden.
Reduce the heat slightly, add the shallots and thyme
and cook for a further 2–3 minutes, stirring occasionally,
until just softened.

Add the beans and vegetable stock, season with a pinch
of salt and plenty of pepper and simmer over a medium
heat for 2–3 minutes, until tender.

Spoon into bowls, drizzle over a little extra olive oil
and serve immediately with crusty bread, plenty of
Parmesan and chopped parsley.

For chunky Italian stew with pancetta, heat
2 tablespoons olive oil in a large saucepan or
flameproof casserole dish over a medium-high heat
and add 200 g (7 oz) cubed pancetta, 1 chopped onion,
2 chopped garlic cloves, 2 sliced celery sticks and
2 diced carrots. Cook for 5–6 minutes, until beginning
to colour. Add 2 diced potatoes, a 400 g (13 oz) can
plum tomatoes, roughly chopped, a 400 g (13 oz)
can cannellini or borlotti beans, rinsed and drained,
1 teaspoon dried oregano and 750 ml (1¼ pints) hot
vegetable or chicken stock. Season generously and
simmer over a medium heat for about 15 minutes
before adding 50 g (2 oz) macaroni or other small
pasta. Cook for a further 5–6 minutes, until the pasta
and vegetables are tender. Ladle into shallow bowls
and serve as above. **Total cooking time 30 minutes.**

pork, red pepper & pea curry

Serves **4**
Total cooking time **30 minutes**

3 tablespoons **vegetable oil**
2 teaspoons **cumin seeds**
2 **onions**, finely chopped
1 tablespoon peeled and
    grated **fresh root ginger**
1 tablespoon grated **garlic**
500 g (1 lb) **minced pork**
2 tablespoons **ground
    coriander**
1 tablespoon **ground cumin**
1 tablespoon **garam masala**
1 **red pepper**, cored,
    deseeded and finely
    chopped
100 g (3½ oz) **frozen peas**
2 **ripe tomatoes**, finely
    chopped
juice of ½ **lime**
salt
handful of chopped **fresh
    coriander**, to garnish

To serve
natural yogurt
warm parathas or **chapattis**
    (optional)

Heat the oil in a large wok or frying pan until hot, add the cumin seeds and stir-fry over a medium heat for 1 minute, then add the onions and stir-fry for a further 3–4 minutes until softened. Add the ginger and garlic and continue to stir-fry for 1 minute.

Add the pork and all the ground spices, season with salt and stir-fry for 8–10 minutes or until the pork is browned and cooked through. Stir in the red pepper, peas and tomatoes and stir-fry for a further 3–4 minutes or until the vegetables are tender. Remove from the heat and stir in the lime juice.

Scatter with chopped coriander and serve with a dollop of yogurt and warm parathas or chapattis, if liked.

For Vietnamese-style pork baguettes, prepare the cooked pork mixture as above. Meanwhile, split 2 warmed baguettes in half lengthways. Divide the cooked pork between the 2 baguettes. Top with 2 sliced tomatoes and a small handful of fresh mint and coriander leaves. Top with the baguette lids, cut each baguette in half and serve. **Total cooking time 10 minutes.**

creamy pork, apple & mustard

Serves **4**
Total cooking time **20 minutes**

2 tablespoons **olive oil**
25 g (1 oz) **butter**
1 large **red onion**, cut into slim
wedges
2 medium **red apples**, cored
and cut into slim wedges
600 g (1 lb 5 oz) **pork fillet**,
thinly sliced
300 ml (½ pint) hot **chicken
stock**
200 ml (7 fl oz) **crème fraîche**
2 tablespoons **Dijon mustard**
2 tablespoons **wholegrain
mustard**
6 tablespoons chopped
parsley
mashed potatoes, to serve

Heat the oil and butter in a large frying pan, add the
onion and apples and cook over a medium-high heat for
5 minutes, turning and stirring occasionally, until golden
and starting to soften. Remove with a slotted spoon and
keep warm.

Add the pork to the pan and cook over a high heat for
5 minutes until golden and cooked through. Return the
onion and apples to the pan with the stock and bring
to the boil. Reduce the heat and simmer for 3 minutes
until the stock has reduced by half, then add the crème
fraîche and mustards and heat through for 2 minutes.

Stir in the parsley, then serve hot with mashed potatoes.

For simple pork, apple & mustard pan-fry, heat
2 tablespoons olive oil and 25 g (1 oz) butter in a
large frying pan, add 1 large cored and roughly chopped
apple and 600 g (1 lb 5 oz) thinly sliced pork fillet and
cook for 5 minutes, stirring occasionally, until golden
and cooked through. Stir in 200 ml (7 fl oz) crème
fraîche and 2 tablespoons wholegrain mustard until well
combined. Scatter with 2 tablespoons chopped parsley
and serve with ready-cooked rice or mashed potatoes.
Total cooking time 10 minutes.

beef & potato balti with spinach

Serves **4**

Total cooking time **30 minutes**

3 tablespoons **vegetable oil**

450 g (14½ oz) **stir-fry beef strips**

1 **red pepper**, cored, deseeded and cut into large chunks

1 **onion**, thickly sliced

250 g (8 oz) **sweet potato**, peeled and diced

500 g (1 lb) **balti cooking sauce**

3 **tomatoes**, cut into wedges

200 g (7 oz) **spinach**, washed and roughly chopped

Heat 2 tablespoons of the oil in a pan set over a medium-high heat and cook the beef for 3–4 minutes, stirring occasionally, until browned and just cooked through. Remove from the pan with a slotted spoon and set aside. Return the pan to the heat.

Add the remaining oil to the pan and cook the pepper, onion and sweet potato for 5–6 minutes, stirring frequently, until lightly coloured and softened.

Stir the balti sauce into the pan with the tomato wedges, then reduce the heat, cover and simmer gently for about 15 minutes or until the vegetables are tender and the sauce has thickened slightly.

Return the beef to the pan, add the spinach and stir over the heat for 1–2 minutes until the beef is hot and the spinach has wilted. Serve immediately.

For curried beef stir-fry with spinach, heat 2 tablespoons oil in a frying pan and cook 450 g (14½ oz) stir-fry beef strips over a high heat for 2 minutes until browned all over. Add 1 thinly sliced onion and cook for 2 minutes. Reduce the heat, stir in 2 tablespoons Madras or balti curry paste and cook for 1 minute. Pour in 400 ml (14 fl oz) reduced-fat coconut milk and 200 ml (7 fl oz) hot beef or vegetable stock. Simmer gently for 2 minutes. Stir in 200 g (7 oz) roughly chopped spinach until just wilted. Serve with naan bread or rice. **Total cooking time 10 minutes.**

sausage & bean cassoulet

Serves **4**
Total cooking time **30 minutes**

2 tablespoons **olive oil**
6 **pork sausages**
1 **onion**, chopped
2 **garlic cloves**, chopped
400 g (13 oz) can **chopped tomatoes**
125 ml (4 fl oz) **chicken stock**
1 **bay leaf**
400 g (13 oz) can **cannellini beans**, rinsed and drained
100 g (3½ oz) **dried breadcrumbs**
handful of chopped **parsley**
salt and **pepper**

Heat 1 tablespoon of the oil in a shallow, flameproof casserole dish. Add the sausages and cook for 5 minutes until starting to turn golden, then add the onion and cook for a further 5 minutes until softened.

Cut the sausages into thick slices, then return to the pan with the garlic and cook for 1 minute. Add the tomatoes, stock, bay leaf and beans, season to taste and bring to the boil. Reduce the heat and simmer for 5 minutes.

Mix together the breadcrumbs and thyme and sprinkle over the cassoulet, then drizzle over the remaining oil. Cook in a preheated oven, 200°C (400°F), Gas Mark 6, for 10–12 minutes until the topping is golden and crisp.

For creamy white bean & sausage bake, mix together 4 sliced cooked smoked sausages, 2 x 400 g (13 oz) cans cannellini beans, rinsed and drained, 125 ml (4 fl oz) crème fraîche, 75 ml (3 fl oz) hot vegetable stock and a handful of chopped thyme. Tip into an ovenproof dish and top with 75 g (3 oz) dried breadcrumbs and 25 g (1 oz) grated Gruyère cheese. Place in a preheated oven, 220°C (425°F), Gas Mark 7, for 15 minutes until golden and bubbling. **Total cooking time 20 minutes.**

sweet & sour pork

Serves **4**
Total cooking time **20 minutes**

1 tablespoon **vegetable oil**
½ **pineapple**, skinned, cored
 and cut into bite-sized
 chunks
1 **onion**, cut into chunks
1 **orange pepper**, cored,
 deseeded and cut into
 chunks
375 g (12 oz) **pork fillet**, cut
 into strips
100 g (3½ oz) **mangetout**,
 halved lengthways
6 tablespoons **tomato
 ketchup**
2 tablespoons **soft light
 brown sugar**
2 tablespoons **white wine** or
 malt vinegar
egg noodles, to serve
 (optional)

Heat the oil in a large, heavy-based frying pan or wok
and stir-fry the pineapple chunks over a very high heat
for 3–4 minutes until browned in places. Remove with
a slotted spoon. Add the onion and orange pepper and
cook over a high heat, stirring frequently, for 5 minutes
until softened. Add the pork strips and stir-fry for
5 minutes until browned and cooked through.

Return the pineapple to the pan with the mangetout
and cook, stirring occasionally, for 2 minutes. Mix the
tomato ketchup, sugar and vinegar together in a jug
and pour over the pork mixture. Toss and cook for a
further 1 minute to heat the sauce through.

Serve immediately, with egg noodles, if liked.

For speedy sweet & sour pork stir-fry, drain the juice
from a 435 g (14 oz) can crushed pineapple and blend
5 tablespoons of juice with 2 tablespoons cornflour,
add 4 tablespoons rice vinegar and 2 tablespoons
each tomato ketchup, dark soy sauce and soft light
brown sugar. Heat 1 tablespoon vegetable oil in a
large frying pan over a high heat and stir-fry 200 g
(7 oz) pork strips for 2 minutes. Add 1 cored, deseeded
and chopped red pepper, stir-fry for 2 minutes, then
add 5 shredded spring onions, the pineapple and the
pineapple juice mixture. Warm through and serve with
noodles. **Total cooking time 10 minutes.**

chorizo, paprika & bean stew

Serves **4**
Total cooking time **30 minutes**

2 tablespoons **olive oil**
200 g (7 oz) **bacon lardons**
500 g (8 oz) **mini cooking
  Spanish chorizo sausages**
1 **onion**, finely chopped
3 x 400 g (13 oz) cans
  **chopped tomatoes with
  herbs**
1 teaspoon **caster sugar**
1 tablespoon **sweet smoked
  paprika**
2 **garlic cloves**, crushed
1 **carrot**, peeled and finely
  diced
1 **celery stick**, finely diced
1 **bay leaf**
1 **chicken stock cube**,
  crumbled
2 x 400 g (13 oz) cans **mixed
  beans**, such as black-eyed
  beans and red kidney beans,
  rinsed and drained
4 tablespoons finely chopped
  flat leaf parsley, plus extra
  to garnish
salt and **pepper**
crusty bread, to serve
  (optional)

Heat the oil in a large heavy-based saucepan, add the bacon and chorizo sausages and cook over a high heat for 3–4 minutes until golden brown.

Stir in the onion, tomatoes, sugar, paprika, garlic, carrot, celery, bay leaf and crumbled stock cube, then reduce the heat to medium and cook, uncovered, for 15–20 minutes.

Add the beans and bring back to the boil, then cook for 2–3 minutes or until piping hot. Season and stir in the parsley.

Ladle into bowls, scatter with extra chopped parsley and serve with crusty bread, if liked.

For quick chorizo, paprika & bean soup, heat 1 tablespoon olive oil in a large saucepan, add 200 g (7 oz) diced chorizo and cook over a high heat for 2–3 minutes. Stir in 1 teaspoon sweet smoked paprika, then add a 600 g (1 lb 5 oz) pot fresh tomato soup and a 400 g (13 oz) can mixed beans, rinsed and drained. Bring to the boil, then reduce the heat to medium and cook for 3–4 minutes or until piping hot. Serve with crusty bread. **Total cooking time 10 minutes.**

cowboy beef & bean casserole

Serves **4**
Total cooking time **30 minutes**

2 tablespoons **olive oil**
1 **onion**, chopped
2 **garlic cloves**, chopped
450 g (14½ oz) **beef**, cut into
    strips
1½ tablespoons **chipotle**
    paste
1 teaspoon **ground cumin**
1½ teaspoons **sweet smoked**
    paprika
175 g (6 oz) **smoked pork**
    sausage, thickly sliced
250 ml (8 fl oz) **lager**
400 g (13 oz) can **chopped**
    tomatoes
2 tablespoons **tomato purée**
400 g (13 oz) can **beans**
    (haricot or kidney), rinsed
    and drained
1 **roasted red pepper** from
    a jar, drained and sliced
    (optional)
Tabasco or **other hot sauce**
salt and **pepper**

To serve
steamed rice
soured cream

Heat the oil in a large saucepan or flameproof casserole dish. Add the onion and garlic and cook for 6–7 minutes, stirring frequently, to soften.

Meanwhile, toss the beef strips in the chipotle paste, cumin and paprika. Add the beef and sausage to the onion mixture and stir over a medium heat for 1 minute. Add the lager, tomatoes, tomato purée, beans, red pepper (if using) and a few shakes of Tabasco. Season, then cover and simmer over a medium-low heat for about 20 minutes, or until rich and thick.

Ladle into dishes and serve with steamed rice and a dollop of soured cream.

For cowboy bean stew, heat 2 tablespoons oil in a frying pan over a medium-high heat. Mix 700 g (1 lb 7 oz) beef stir-fry strips with the chipotle paste and spices, as above, and stir-fry for 5–6 minutes, until the meat is browned. Add 2 x 400 g (13 oz) cans baked beans, heated, 1 tablespoon Worcestershire sauce and a few shakes of Tabasco. Serve with jacket potatoes or steamed rice and a dollop of soured cream, as above. **Total cooking time 10 minutes.**

bacon, tomato & bean salad

Serves **4**
Total cooking time **10 minutes**

3 tablespoons **olive** or
  vegetable oil
6 **back bacon rashers**,
  chopped
2 **garlic cloves**, chopped
1 teaspoon **paprika**
3 **tomatoes**, deseeded and
  diced
2 x 400 g (13 oz) cans **butter
  beans**, rinsed and drained
2 tablespoons chopped
  parsley
2 tablespoons **lemon juice**

Heat the oil in a large frying pan and cook the bacon over a medium heat for 6–7 minutes, stirring occasionally, until crisp and golden. Stir in the garlic and paprika for the final minute of cooking, then add the tomatoes, butter beans, parsley and lemon juice and toss to warm through.

Spoon into 4 dishes and serve immediately.

For tomato, bacon & butter bean stew, heat 3 tablespoons olive or vegetable oil in a large saucepan and cook 6 rashers of roughly chopped back bacon over a medium heat for 4–5 minutes until golden, then add 1 chopped onion and cook for a further 4–5 minutes until softened. Stir 2 large carrots, peeled and diced, 2 chopped garlic cloves and 1 teaspoon paprika into the pan and cook for 1–2 minutes until the garlic is softened. Add a 400 g (13 oz) can butter beans, rinsed and drained, a 400 g (13 oz) can chopped tomatoes and 250 ml (8 fl oz) hot vegetable stock. Bring to the boil, then cover, reduce the heat and simmer gently for about 15 minutes until thickened. Scatter over 2 tablespoons chopped fresh coriander and serve with couscous. **Total cooking time 30 minutes.**

beef, pumpkin & prune stew

Serves **4**

Total cooking time **30 minutes**

2 tablespoons **olive oil**

1 **garlic clove**, chopped

1 large **onion**, chopped

500 g (1 lb) peeled, deseeded
and cubed **pumpkin**

600 g (1 lb 5 oz) **beef steak**
(such as sirloin, rump or
frying), cubed

2 teaspoons **ground
coriander**

2 teaspoons **ground cumin**

150 g (5 oz) **ready-to-eat soft
dried prunes**

2 x 400 g (13 oz) cans
chopped tomatoes

450 ml (¾ pint) hot **beef
stock**

100 g (3½ oz) **fresh
coriander**, chopped

To serve

couscous

natural yogurt

Heat the oil in a large saucepan or flameproof casserole, add the garlic, onion, pumpkin and beef and cook over a high heat for 5–10 minutes until the beef is browned and the pumpkin is golden. Add the spices and cook for a further 1 minute.

Add the prunes, tomatoes and stock and bring to the boil, then reduce the heat, cover and simmer for 15 minutes, stirring occasionally, until the stew is thickened and the meat and vegetables are cooked through.

Scatter over the chopped coriander and stir through. Serve with couscous, topped with spoonfuls of yogurt.

For speedy beef, tomato & prune pan-fry, heat 2 tablespoons olive oil in a large frying pan, add 600 g (1 lb 5 oz) thinly sliced beef frying steak and cook over a high heat for 2 minutes. Add 2 teaspoons ground coriander, 2 teaspoons ground cumin and 8 chopped tomatoes and cook for a further 2–3 minutes until softened. Serve hot, scattered with 12 roughly chopped ready-to-eat dried prunes and 2 tablespoons chopped fresh coriander. **Total cooking time 10 minutes.**

roast pork with fennel & lemon

Serves **4**

Total cooking time **30 minutes**

2 x 375 g (12 oz) **pork tenderloins**

2 tablespoons **olive oil**

2 **lemons**

750 g (1½ lb) small **new potatoes**, halved

1 **fennel bulb**, sliced

3–4 **sage leaves**

salt and **pepper**

Rub the pork with a little of the oil and place in a large, shallow roasting tin. Finely grate the rind of 1 lemon and sprinkle over the pork with salt and lots of pepper.

Scatter the potatoes around the pork and drizzle over the remaining oil. Place in a preheated oven, 220°C (425°F), Gas Mark 7, for 10 minutes.

Cut the other lemon into wedges and add to the roasting tin with the fennel and sage leaves. Return to the oven for 15 minutes until the meat and potatoes are cooked through.

For fennel & lemon porkballs with cannellini beans,

mix 400 g (13 oz) minced pork with the finely grated rind of 1 lemon, 1 teaspoon crushed fennel seeds, ½ finely chopped red chilli, 50 g (2 oz) fresh white breadcrumbs and 1 egg yolk. Season to taste and use wet hands to shape into 12 balls. Heat 1 tablespoon olive oil in a flameproof casserole dish. Fry the balls for 5 minutes until golden, then add 250 ml (8 fl oz) hot chicken stock and simmer for 5 minutes. Add 125 g (4 oz) halved cherry tomatoes and a 400 g (13 oz) can cannellini beans, rinsed and drained. Cook for a further 5 minutes until heated through, then serve scattered with chopped basil. **Total cooking time 20 minutes.**

eggs with merguez sausage

Serves **4**
Total cooking time **20 minutes**

2 tablespoons **olive oil**
1 **onion**, finely sliced
1 **red chilli**, deseeded and
    finely chopped
1 **garlic clove**, crushed
300 g (10 oz) **merguez
    sausages**, roughly chopped
1 teaspoon **dried oregano**
400 g (13 oz) can **cherry
    tomatoes**
100 ml (3½ fl oz) **passata
    with herbs**
200 g (7 oz) **roasted mixed
    peppers** from a jar, drained
    and roughly chopped
4 **eggs**
salt and **pepper**
4 tablespoons finely chopped
    fresh coriander, to garnish

Heat the oil in a large frying pan, add the onion, red chilli, garlic, merguez sausages and oregano and fry gently for about 5 minutes or until the onion is softened. Add the tomatoes, passata and peppers and cook for a further 5 minutes. If the sauce looks dry, add a splash of water.

Season well, then make 4 hollows in the mixture, break an egg into each and cover the pan. Cook for 5 minutes or until the eggs are set.

Divide between 4 serving plates, scatter with chopped coriander and serve immediately.

For Merguez sausage & tomato tortilla, heat 2 tablespoons sunflower oil in a medium ovenproof frying pan, add 1 chopped onion, 200 g (7 oz) roughly chopped merguez sausages, 1 deseeded and chopped red chilli and 1 chopped garlic clove and cook over a medium heat for 3–4 minutes. Add 2 chopped tomatoes and cook for a further 3–4 minutes. Lightly beat 6 eggs in a bowl, then season and pour into the pan. Cook over a medium heat for 10–12 minutes or until the base is set, then place the pan under a preheated medium-hot grill and cook for 4–5 minutes or until the top is golden and set. Cut the tortilla into wedges and serve. **Total cooking time 30 minutes.**

bacon, pea & courgette risotto

Serves **4**
Total cooking time **30 minutes**

50 g (2 oz) **butter**
150 g (5 oz) **streaky bacon**,
   diced
300 g (10 oz) **risotto rice**
100 ml (3½ fl oz) **dry white
   wine** (optional)
900 ml (1½ pints) hot **chicken**
   or **vegetable stock** (add an
   extra 100 ml (3½ fl oz) if not
   using wine)
2 **courgettes**, about 325 g
   (11 oz) total weight, coarsely
   grated
200 g (7 oz) **frozen peas**,
   defrosted
1 small bunch of **basil**,
   shredded (optional)
salt and **pepper**
grated **Parmesan cheese**,
   to serve

Melt the butter in a large frying pan or saucepan
and cook the diced bacon over a medium heat for
6–7 minutes until golden. Remove half of the bacon
with a slotted spoon and set aside.

Stir in the risotto rice and pour in the white wine, if
using, and hot stock. Bring to the boil, then simmer
gently for 15–18 minutes, stirring as often as possible,
until the rice is tender and creamy. Stir in the grated
courgette and defrosted peas for the final 2–3 minutes
of cooking time.

Season, then spoon the risotto into 4 bowls. Scatter
over the reserved bacon and shredded basil, if using.
Serve sprinkled with grated Parmesan cheese.

For lazy pea & bacon noodles, heat 50 g (2 oz)
butter in a large saucepan and cook 200 g (7 oz)
finely chopped bacon over a medium-high heat, stirring
occasionally, for 4–5 minutes until lightly golden. Pour
over 600 ml (1 pint) boiling ham, chicken or vegetable
stock, 2 tablespoons barbecue sauce, 200 g (7 oz)
frozen peas and 400 g (13 oz) fresh noodles. Cover
and simmer for 3–4 minutes until the peas and noodles
are tender. Lift out the noodles and heap into bowls,
then pour over the soup to serve. **Total cooking time
10 minutes.**

spicy beef & squash stew

Serves **4**

Total cooking time **30 minutes**

2 tablespoons **vegetable oil**

2 large **beef steaks**, cut into chunks

1 **onion**, finely chopped

1 small **butternut squash**, peeled and cut into chunks

1 **red chilli**, deseeded and chopped

1 teaspoon **ground cumin**

1 tablespoon **tomato purée**

400 g (13 oz) can **cherry tomatoes**

150 g (5 oz) **canned sweetcorn kernels**

handful of chopped **fresh coriander**, to garnish

Heat half the oil in a large, heavy-based saucepan. Add the steak and cook over a high heat for about 3 minutes until browned, then remove from the pan and set aside.

Add the remaining oil to the pan with the onion and squash and cook for 5 minutes until softened. Stir in the chilli and cumin and cook for 30 seconds, then add the tomato purée and tomatoes and simmer for 15 minutes.

Return the beef to the pan with the sweetcorn and heat through. Serve scattered with the coriander.

For beef, tomato & beans with nacho topping, heat 1 tablespoon oil in a large, flameproof frying pan. Add 1 finely chopped onion and cook for 2 minutes, then stir in 300 g (10 oz) minced beef. Cook for 5 minutes until golden, then add 1 teaspoon each of ground coriander and cumin. Stir in a 200 g (7 oz) can chopped tomatoes and simmer for 10 minutes, topping up with a little water if necessary. Add 200 g (7 oz) canned kidney beans, rinsed and drained, and heat through. Arrange 75 g (3 oz) tortilla chips on top of the stew and scatter with 50 g (2 oz) grated Cheddar cheese. Cook under a preheated hot grill for 1–2 minutes until the cheese melts. Serve with soured cream, guacamole and salsa. **Total cooking time 20 minutes.**

caramelized parsnips

Serves **2**
Total cooking time **20 minutes**

625 g (1¼ lb) **parsnips**,
　scrubbed or peeled
50 g (2 oz) **butter**
175 g (6 oz) diced **bacon**
3 tablespoons **caster sugar**
50 g (2 oz) **pine nuts**
5 tablespoons chopped **thyme
　leaves**

Cut the parsnips in half widthways, then cut the chunky tops into quarters lengthways and the slim bottom halves in half lengthways.

Heat the butter in a large wok or frying pan, add the bacon and parsnips and cook over a medium heat for 15 minutes, turning and tossing occasionally, until the parsnips are golden and softened and the bacon is crisp.

Add the caster sugar and pine nuts and cook for a further 2–3 minutes until lightly caramelized. Toss with the thyme and serve.

For bacon, pine nut & parsnip rosti, grate 350 g (11½ oz) peeled parsnips into a bowl and mix with 50 g (2 oz) ready-cooked bacon rashers, snipped into small pieces, and 2 tablespoons chopped parsley. Divide the mixture and squeeze together to form 4 balls, then flatten into patties. Heat 50 g (2 oz) butter in a large frying pan, add the patties and cook over a high heat for 2 minutes on each side until golden. Serve hot with a green salad and sprinkled with pine nuts. **Total cooking time 10 minutes.**

spicy lamb & vegetable stew

Serves **4**

Total cooking time **30 minutes**

1 tablespoon **sunflower oil**

600 g (1 lb 5 oz) **lamb neck fillet**, cut into 2 cm (¾ inch) cubes

1 **onion**, chopped

1 **garlic clove**, crushed

1 teaspoon peeled and grated **fresh root ginger**

2 tablespoons **medium curry paste**

1 large **potato**, peeled and cut into 2 cm (¾ inch) cubes

1 large **carrot**, peeled and cut into 2 cm (¾ inch) cubes

400 ml (14 fl oz) hot **lamb stock**

200 ml (7 fl oz) **coconut milk**

200 g (7 oz) **frozen peas**

handful of chopped **fresh coriander**, to garnish

steamed **rice**, to serve (optional)

Heat the oil in a large heavy-based saucepan, add the lamb, onion, garlic and ginger and cook over a high heat for 3–4 minutes, stirring frequently, until the lamb is browned and the onion is softened. Reduce the heat to medium, add the curry paste and cook, stirring, for a further 1–2 minutes.

Stir in the potato, carrot, stock and coconut milk and bring to the boil. Cook, uncovered, for 15–20 minutes or until the lamb and vegetables are tender. Stir in the peas 3 minutes before the end of the cooking time.

Ladle into bowls, scatter with the coriander and serve with steamed rice, if liked.

For spicy lamb & vegetable curry, heat 2 tablespoons sunflower oil in a large wok or frying pan until hot. Add 1 chopped onion, 2 chopped garlic cloves and 1 teaspoon peeled and grated fresh root ginger and stir-fry over a high heat for 1–2 minutes, then add 600 g (1 lb 5 oz) minced lamb, 3 tablespoons medium curry paste, 200 g (7 oz) each peeled potatoes and carrots, cut into 1 cm (½ inch) cubes, and stir-fry for a further 1–2 minutes until the lamb is browned. Pour in 200 ml (7 fl oz) coconut milk and cook, uncovered, over a medium heat for 10–12 minutes, stirring frequently, until the lamb and vegetables are tender. Season, then serve immediately with steamed rice or crusty bread. **Total cooking time 20 minutes.**

west indian beef & bean stew

Serves **4**
Total cooking time **30 minutes**

3 tablespoons **sunflower oil**
800 g (1¾ lb) **minced beef**
6 whole **cloves**
1 **onion**, finely chopped
2 tablespoons **medium curry powder**
2 **carrots**, peeled and cut into 1 cm (½ inch) cubes
2 **celery sticks**, diced
1 tablespoon **thyme** leaves
2 **garlic cloves**, crushed
4 tablespoons **tomato purée**
600 ml (1 pint) hot **beef stock**
1 large **potato**, peeled and cut into 1 cm (½ inch) cubes
200 g (7 oz) can **black beans**, rinsed and drained
200 g (7 oz) can **black-eyed beans**, rinsed and drained
salt and **pepper**
lemon wedges, to serve

Heat the oil in a large heavy-based saucepan, add the beef and fry, stirring, over a medium-high heat for 5–6 minutes or until browned.

Add the cloves, onion and curry powder and cook for 2–3 minutes until the onions are beginning to soften, then stir in the carrots, celery, thyme, garlic and tomato purée.

Pour in the beef stock to just cover the meat and stir well, then add the potato and beans and bring to the boil. Reduce the heat slightly and simmer for 20 minutes, uncovered, or until the potatoes and beef are tender, then season to taste.

Ladle into bowls and serve with lemon wedges.

For curried beef & black bean pilau, heat 2 tablespoons sunflower oil in a large wok or frying pan until hot, add 500 g (1 lb) minced beef and 1 tablespoon medium curry paste and stir-fry over a high heat for 2–3 minutes until browned. Add 100 ml (3½ fl oz) coconut milk, reduce the heat to medium and simmer gently for 6–8 minutes or until most of the liquid has been absorbed and the beef is cooked through. Stir in 500 g (1 lb) ready-cooked long-grain or basmati rice and 200 g (7 oz) can black beans, rinsed and drained, and heat through for 2–3 minutes or until piping hot. Season, then serve immediately. **Total cooking time 20 minutes.**

pork & paprika goulash

Serves **4**

Total cooking time **30 minutes**

2 tablespoons **vegetable oil**

400 g (13 oz) **pork loin**, cubed

1 **onion**, sliced

2 teaspoons **smoked paprika**

400 g (13 oz) can **chopped tomatoes**

500 g (1 lb) **potatoes**, peeled and diced

4 tablespoons **soured cream**

salt and **pepper**

handful of chopped **parsley**, to garnish

Heat half the oil in a deep frying pan. Add the pork, season to taste and cook for 5 minutes until browned all over. Remove from the pan and set aside. Add the remaining oil to the pan along with the onion and cook for 5 minutes until softened.

Stir in the paprika, then add the tomatoes and potatoes. Season to taste, bring to the boil, then reduce the heat and simmer for 10 minutes.

Return the pork to the pan and cook for a further 5 minutes until the pork and potatoes are cooked through. Divide between serving bowls, top with the soured cream and serve sprinkled with parsley.

For crispy paprika pork chops with roasted peppers, mix 75 g (3 oz) dried breadcrumbs with the finely grated rind of ½ lemon and 2 teaspoons smoked paprika. Dip 4 pork chops into olive oil, then press into the breadcrumb mixture and season to taste. Arrange the chops on a baking sheet with 2 cored, deseeded and sliced red peppers. Place in a preheated oven, 220°C (425°F), Gas Mark 7, for 15 minutes until the pork is cooked through, then serve with a green salad. **Total cooking time 20 minutes.**

fish & seafood

crispy fish pie

Serves **4**
Total cooking time **30 minutes**

butter, for greasing
200 g (7 oz) **frozen spinach**
400 g (13 oz) **skinless
 salmon fillet**, cubed
250 g (8 oz) **skinless smoked
 haddock fillet**, cubed
4 eggs
100 ml (3½ fl oz) **crème
 fraîche**
2 tablespoons **boiling water**
50 g (2 oz) **dried breadcrumbs**
salt and **pepper**

Lightly grease an ovenproof dish. Place the spinach in a sieve and pour over boiling water from the kettle until it has defrosted. Lay the spinach on a sheet of kitchen paper and squeeze to get rid of excess water.

Arrange the spinach in the ovenproof dish and place the fish on top. Make 4 small holes between the fish pieces and crack an egg into each one.

Mix the crème fraîche with the measurement water and season to taste. Pour over the fish, then scatter with the breadcrumbs. Place in a preheated oven, 200°C (400°F), Gas Mark 6, for 25 minutes or until golden and bubbling and the fish is cooked through.

For fish pots with crispy topping, divide 250 g (8 oz) skinless smoked haddock fillet, cut into small pieces, between 4 ramekins. Stir together 75 ml (3 fl oz) crème fraîche, a handful of chopped chives and 2 tablespoons water, then stir into the fish. Place in a preheated oven, 180°C (350°F), Gas Mark 4, for 5–7 minutes. Crack an egg on top of each ramekin, top with a sprinkling of dried breadcrumbs and a drizzle of melted butter, then return to the oven for a further 10–12 minutes until the eggs are set. Serve with crusty bread. **Total cooking time 20 minutes.**

rich tomato, wine & fish stew

Serves **4**
Total cooking time **10 minutes**

2 x 400 g (13 oz) jars **tomato sauce with peppers and onion**
150 ml (¼ pint) **white wine**
1 tablespoon **olive oil**
375 g (12 oz) **skinless white fish fillets**, torn or cut into chunks
175 g (6 oz) **raw peeled prawns**
25 g (1 oz) **parsley**, chopped
pepper
crusty bread, to serve (optional)

Place the tomato sauce, wine and oil in a large, heavy-based saucepan and bring to the boil.

Reduce the heat, add the fish and prawns and simmer for 7 minutes until the fish is opaque and cooked through and the prawns have turned pink.

Add the parsley and season with pepper, then serve in bowls with warm crusty bread, if liked.

For Mediterranean fish stew with chunky vegetables, heat 1 tablespoon olive oil in a large, deep frying pan and cook 2 trimmed and chunkily chopped courgettes, 1 Romero red pepper and 1 yellow pepper, each cored, deseeded and cut into chunks, and 1 finely chopped red onion over a medium heat, stirring occasionally, for 8–10 minutes until softened. Add 500 g (1 lb) mixed skinless white fish fillets, cut into chunks, 175 g (6 oz) cooked peeled prawns, 2 x 400 g (13 oz) jars tomato pasta sauce and 300 ml (½ pint) white wine and cook, stirring very gently occasionally, for 10 minutes or until the fish is cooked through. Stir in 100 g (3½ oz) pitted black olives and serve in bowls topped with 75 g (3 oz) ready-made croûtons. **Total cooking time 30 minutes.**

smoked haddock kedgeree

Serves **4**
Total cooking time **30 minutes**

1 tablespoon **vegetable oil**
25 g (1 oz) **butter**
1 **onion**, finely chopped
1 **garlic clove**, crushed
1 teaspoon finely grated **fresh root ginger**
1 teaspoon **cumin seeds**
½ teaspoon **coriander seeds**
1 teaspoon **curry powder**
½ teaspoon **ground turmeric**
300 g (10 oz) **basmati rice**
650 ml (1 pint 2 fl oz) hot **chicken** or **fish stock**
300 g (10 oz) **skinless smoked haddock fillet**
75 g (3 oz) **frozen peas**
1 **red chilli**, deseeded and chopped
handful of chopped **fresh coriander**
salt and **pepper**
mango chutney, to serve

Heat the oil and butter in a large saucepan. Add the onion and cook for 5 minutes, then stir in the garlic and ginger and cook for 1 minute. Add the cumin and coriander seeds and cook for 30 seconds, then stir in the curry powder, turmeric and rice and cook for a further 1 minute.

Pour in the stock and cook for 5 minutes. Place the fish fillet on top of the rice and cook for a further 5 minutes. By this time, most of the stock should have boiled away. Add the peas, cover the pan tightly with a lid, turn down the heat as low as it will go and cook for 5–7 minutes until the rice is cooked through.

Use a fork to gently break up the fish, stir the fish and peas into the rice and season to taste. Scatter with the chilli and coriander and serve with mango chutney.

For smoked haddock, rice & spinach soup, cook

1 chopped onion in 1 tablespoon oil for 5 minutes, then add 100 g (3½ oz) basmati rice, 1.5 litres (2½ pints) hot chicken or fish stock and a pinch of saffron threads. Simmer for 10 minutes, then add 300 g (10 oz) skinless smoked haddock fillet and cook for 3 minutes until starting to break up. Add 100 ml (3½ fl oz) single cream and 100 g (3½ oz) baby spinach leaves and heat through until wilted. **Total cooking time 20 minutes.**

clam, kale & butter bean stew

Serves **4**
Total cooking time **20 minutes**

1 tablespoon **olive oil**
50 g (2 oz) **chorizo**, chopped
1 **onion**, finely chopped
2 **garlic cloves**, chopped
1 teaspoon **tomato purée**
50 ml (2 fl oz) **dry white wine**
200 ml (7 fl oz) hot **chicken stock**
75 g (3 oz) **kale**, chopped
500 g (1 lb) **clams**, rinsed and drained
200 g (7 oz) can **butter beans**, rinsed and drained
salt and **pepper**

Heat the oil in a large saucepan or flameproof casserole dish. Add the chorizo and cook for 1 minute until starting to release its oil. Add the onion and cook for a further 5 minutes until softened, then stir in the garlic and tomato purée and cook for 1 minute.

Pour in the wine and let it bubble away until reduced by half. Add the stock and kale and cook for 5 minutes.

Add the clams, cover and cook for 3 minutes, then stir in the beans. Cover and cook for a further 3 minutes until the clams have opened, discarding any that have not. Season to taste and serve.

For stir-fried clams & kale in black bean sauce,

heat 2 tablespoons oil in a wok. Add 2 sliced garlic cloves and cook for a few seconds, then add 150 g (5 oz) chopped kale and stir-fry for 1–2 minutes. Add ½ finely chopped chilli and 2 teaspoons finely grated fresh root ginger and stir in, then add 500 g (1 lb) clams, rinsed and drained, and 75 ml (3 fl oz) black bean sauce. Add a splash of water, cover and cook for 5 minutes until the clams have opened, discarding any that have not. Scatter with 1 sliced spring onion before serving with ready-cooked rice. **Total cooking time 10 minutes.**

creamy, curried mussel soup

Serves **4**

Total cooking time **20 minutes**

1 tablespoon **butter**

2 **shallots**, thinly sliced

2 **garlic cloves**, crushed

1 teaspoon peeled and finely
grated **fresh root ginger**

2 large **red chillies**, deseeded
and finely diced

1 teaspoon **medium curry
powder**

1 large pinch of **saffron
threads**

100 ml (3½ fl oz) **dry white
wine**

400 ml (14 fl oz) hot
vegetable stock

1 kg (2¼ lb) **live mussels**,
scrubbed and debearded

200 ml (7 fl oz) **double cream**

6 tablespoons finely chopped
fresh coriander

salt and **pepper**

crusty bread, to serve
(optional)

Heat the butter in a large wok or frying pan, add the
shallots, garlic, ginger, red chillies and curry powder and
stir-fry over a high heat for 1 minute. Add the saffron,
white wine and stock and bring to the boil, then reduce
the heat to medium and cook for 1–2 minutes.

Add the mussels to the pan, discarding any that are
cracked or don't shut when tapped, and cover tightly.
Increase the heat to high and cook for 2–3 minutes,
shaking the pan occasionally, until the mussels have
opened. Discard any that remain closed. Remove the
mussels with a slotted spoon and set aside.

Pour the cream into the stock mixture and bring back
to the boil, then reduce the heat and simmer gently,
uncovered, for 5–6 minutes. Return the mussels to
the pan, stir in the coriander and season to taste.

Ladle into soup bowls and serve with crusty bread,
if liked.

For curried smoked mussel omelette, whisk together
4 eggs and 2 teaspoons hot curry powder in a bowl,
then season with salt. Heat 2 tablespoons butter in
a large frying pan and add the egg mixture, swirling
to coat evenly. Cook for 1–2 minutes and then add a
drained 85 g (3 oz) can smoked mussels in olive oil
down the centre. Fold the egg mixture over the mussels.
Flip to seal and cook for 1–2 minutes. Keep warm while
you repeat the recipe, to make 2 omelettes in total.
Divide each omelette in two and serve one half per
person. **Total cooking time 10 minutes.**

baked tuna with ratatouille

Serves **4**

Total cooking time **30 minutes**

1 **onion**, cut into wedges

1 **aubergine**, cut into chunks

1 **red pepper**, cored, deseeded and cut into chunks

1 **courgette**, thickly sliced

4 **tomatoes**, quartered

5 tablespoons **olive oil**

2 **garlic cloves**, crushed

1 tablespoon **sherry vinegar**

4 **tuna steaks**

salt and **pepper**

handful of chopped **basil**, to garnish

Toss the vegetables with 3 tablespoons of the oil, arrange in a shallow roasting dish and season to taste. Place in a preheated oven, 200°C (400°F), Gas Mark 6, for 15 minutes, turning occasionally, until lightly charred.

Mix the remaining oil with the garlic and vinegar and stir into the vegetables. Arrange the tuna steaks in the dish and season well. Return to the oven for a further 12–15 minutes until the tuna is cooked. Serve immediately, scattered with the basil.

For roasted tuna with ratatouille topping, rub

1 tablespoon olive oil over 4 tuna steaks and place in a shallow roasting tin. Scatter 75 g (3 oz) halved cherry tomatoes, 1 cored, deseeded and chopped red pepper, 1 sliced garlic clove and 1 tablespoon capers, rinsed and drained, over the fish, season well and drizzle over 1 tablespoon olive oil. Place in a preheated oven, 200°C (400°F), Gas Mark 6, for 12–15 minutes until the vegetables are lightly charred and the tuna is cooked. Sprinkle with chopped basil before serving with crusty bread. **Total cooking time 20 minutes.**

salmon, pea & dill tortilla

Serves **4**
Total cooking time **30 minutes**

400 g (13 oz) **potatoes**,
  peeled and thickly sliced
150 g (5 oz) **skinless salmon
  fillet**
6 **eggs**, beaten
handful of **dill**, chopped
100 g (3½ oz) **frozen peas**
1 **spring onion**, sliced
1 tablespoon **vegetable oil**
salt and **pepper**
mixed salad leaves, to serve

Cook the potatoes in a saucepan of lightly salted boiling water for 10 minutes until tender, then drain.

Meanwhile, place the salmon in a small saucepan. Cover with boiling water and leave to simmer for 7 minutes until the fish flakes easily. Drain, then break into large flakes.

Mix together the eggs, dill, peas and spring onion, then season. Heat the oil in a 20 cm (8 inch) nonstick frying pan. Stir the potatoes and salmon into the egg mixture, then tip into the pan. Cook over a very low heat for 10–15 minutes until just set. Cut into wedges and serve with a mixed leaf salad.

For pea & salmon omelettes, cook 25 g (1 oz) frozen peas in boiling water for 3 minutes until cooked through, then drain. Beat 4 eggs together with some dill. Heat 15 g (½ oz) butter in small frying pan. Add a quarter of the egg mixture and swirl around the pan. Cook for 1 minute until the mixture is starting to set, then sprinkle over 1 teaspoon grated Parmesan cheese, a few of the peas and a slice of smoked salmon, cut into strips. Fold over the omelette and keep warm while you repeat with the remaining egg mixture to make 4 omelettes in total. **Total cooking time 10 minutes.**

king prawn & sweet potato curry

Serves **4**
Total cooking time **30 minutes**

2 tablespoons **vegetable oil**
1 large **onion**, chopped
2 **garlic cloves**, sliced
1 tablespoon peeled and
　chopped **fresh root ginger**
1 **green chilli**, deseeded and
　thinly sliced
3 tablespoons **mild curry
　paste**
400 g (13 oz) **sweet potato**,
　peeled and diced
400 ml (14 fl oz) **coconut milk**
250 ml (8 fl oz) **vegetable
　stock**
small handful of **curry leaves**
400 g (13 oz) **raw peeled
　king prawns**
100 g (3½ oz) **frozen leaf
　spinach**, defrosted and
　drained
handful of chopped **fresh
　coriander**
warm **naan bread**, to serve

Heat the oil in a large, deep-sided frying pan or wok and cook the onion over a medium-high heat for 3–4 minutes, until beginning to colour. Add the garlic, ginger and chilli and stir-fry for a further 2 minutes. Reduce the heat slightly and add the curry paste, stirring for 1–2 minutes.

Add the sweet potato dice, tossing them to coat, then add the coconut milk, stock and curry leaves. Simmer gently for 12–15 minutes, until the sweet potato is almost tender.

Stir the prawns and spinach into the curry and heat for 2–3 minutes, until the prawns are just cooked through and pink.

Sprinkle over the chopped coriander, spoon the curry into dishes and serve immediately with naan bread.

For curried prawn broth, heat 2 tablespoons oil in a large saucepan and fry 2 sliced banana shallots and 2 sliced garlic cloves over a high heat, stirring, for 2–3 minutes. Reduce the heat, add 1 tablespoon korma curry paste and stir for 1 minute. Pour 1 litre (1¾ pints) hot vegetable stock into the pan. Add 300 g (10 oz) raw peeled king prawns, 250 g (8 oz) cooked long-grain rice, 2 seeded and diced tomatoes and 2 tablespoons chopped coriander. Simmer for 2–3 minutes, until the prawns are cooked through, then ladle into bowls to serve. **Total cooking time 10 minutes.**

rich tomato & fish stew

Serves **4**
Total cooking time **20 minutes**

1 tablespoon **olive oil**
1 **onion**, thinly sliced
1 **garlic clove**, chopped
2 **tomatoes**, roughly chopped
400 g (13 oz) can **chopped tomatoes**
4 tablespoons **sun-dried tomato paste**
150 ml (¼ pint) **white wine**
375 g (12 oz) **mixed skinless fish fillets**, cut into chunks
175 g (6 oz) **raw peeled prawns**
5 tablespoons chopped **thyme**
75 g (3 oz) **pitted black olives**
pepper
warm **crusty bread**, to serve

Heat the oil in a large, heavy-based saucepan and cook the onion and garlic over a medium heat, stirring frequently, for 3–4 minutes until softened. Add the fresh tomatoes and cook, stirring, for 2–3 minutes, then add the canned tomatoes, tomato paste and wine. Bring to the boil and cook over a high heat for 5 minutes until the sauce is thick.

Stir the fish chunks and prawns into the tomato mixture, then reduce the heat, cover and simmer for 7–8 minutes until the fish is opaque and cooked through and the prawns have turned pink. Stir through the thyme and black olives and season with pepper to taste.

Serve in serving bowls with warm crusty bread to mop up the juices.

For instant fish stew, heat 1 tablespoon olive oil in a heavy-based saucepan and cook 1 finely chopped onion with a squeeze of garlic paste over a medium heat, stirring, for 3 minutes. Add a 400 g (13 oz) can lobster bisque, a 200 g (7 oz) can chopped tomatoes, 175 g (6 oz) mixed skinless fish fillets, cut into chunks, and 175 g (6 oz) cooked peeled prawns and cook over a high heat for 7 minutes until the seafood is cooked through. Serve with crusty bread. **Total cooking time 10 minutes.**

seafood paella

Serves **4**

Total cooking time **30 minutes**

1 tablespoon **olive oil**

75 g (3 oz) **chorizo**, thickly sliced

1 **onion**, finely chopped

1 **red pepper**, cored, deseeded and chopped

2 **garlic cloves**, chopped

300 g (10 oz) **paella rice**

1 teaspoon **smoked paprika**

pinch of **saffron threads**

800 ml (1 pint 7 fl oz) hot **chicken stock**

300 g (10 oz) **live mussels**, scrubbed and debearded

8 **cooked king prawns, shells on**

100 g (3½ oz) **raw squid rings**

75 g (3 oz) **frozen peas**

salt and **pepper**

Heat the oil in a large, heavy-based saucepan. Add the chorizo to the pan and cook for about 2 minutes until starting to brown. Remove from the pan with a slotted spoon and set aside.

Add the onion and pepper to the pan and cook for 3 minutes, then stir in the garlic and cook for 1 minute. Add the rice and stir until well coated.

Sprinkle over the paprika and saffron, return the chorizo to the pan, then pour over the hot stock. Bring to the boil, then simmer, uncovered, for 15 minutes. Add the mussels, cover the pan and cook for 3 minutes.

Stir in the prawns, squid and peas and cook for a further 2 minutes until the rice is tender (add a drizzle of hot water around the edge of the pan if still a little firm) and the mussels have opened – discard any that remain closed, then season to taste and serve.

For saffron & fennel seafood, heat 2 tablespoons olive oil in a large saucepan. Cook 1 finely chopped fennel bulb for 2 minutes. Add 150 ml (¼ pint) dry white wine, a good pinch of saffron threads and 500 g (1 lb) live mussels, scrubbed and debearded. Cover and cook for 3 minutes. Add 8 cooked peeled large prawns and 100 g (3½ oz) raw squid rings. Cook for 2 minutes. Discard any mussels that remain closed. **Total cooking time 10 minutes**.

monkfish & mixed pepper stew

Serves **4**

Total cooking time **20 minutes**

2 tablespoons **vegetable oil**

2 **onions**, finely chopped

2 tablespoons **medium** or **hot curry powder**

1 teaspoon **ground turmeric**

900 g (2 lb) **monkfish tail**, cut into bite-sized pieces

2 **garlic cloves**, chopped

1 teaspoon peeled and finely grated **fresh root ginger**

½ teaspoon **tamarind paste**

1 tablespoon **thyme leaves**

1 **star anise**

450 ml (¾ pint) hot **fish stock**

1 **red pepper**, cored, deseeded and cut into 3 cm (1 inch) pieces

1 **yellow pepper**, cored, deseeded and cut into 3 cm (1 inch) pieces

steamed **rice**, to serve (optional)

Heat the oil in a heavy-based saucepan, add the onions and cook over a medium heat, stirring occasionally, for 2–3 minutes until softened. Stir in the curry powder and turmeric and cook for a further 1 minute until fragrant.

Add the remaining ingredients and stir together well. Bring to a simmer, then reduce the heat to low and cook, uncovered, for 8–10 minutes or until the fish is cooked through and the peppers are tender.

Ladle into bowls and serve with steamed rice, if liked.

For Chinese monkfish & mixed pepper stir-fry,

core, deseeded and finely slice 1 red pepper and 1 yellow pepper. Heat 2 tablespoons sunflower oil in a large wok or frying pan until hot, add the peppers and 600 g (1 lb 5 oz) monkfish tail, cubed, and stir-fry over a high heat for 2–3 minutes. Add a 120 g (4 oz) sachet oyster and spring onion stir-fry sauce and fry for a further 2–3 minutes or until the fish is cooked through and piping hot. Serve immediately with steamed rice. **Total cooking time 10 minutes.**

mussels in a coconut broth

Serves **4**

Total cooking time **20 minutes**

1 tablespoon **vegetable oil**

1 **shallot**, finely chopped

1 **garlic clove**, sliced

1 **red chilli**, deseeded and chopped

2 **lime leaves**, shredded

125 ml (4 fl oz) **coconut milk**

125 ml (4 fl oz) **water**

1 **lemon grass stalk**

1 tablespoon **Thai fish sauce**

1 tablespoon **soft brown sugar**

1 kg (2 lb) **live mussels**, scrubbed and debearded

handful of chopped **fresh coriander**, to serve

Heat the oil in a large saucepan, add the shallot and cook for 2 minutes. Stir in the garlic, chilli and lime leaves and cook for 1 minute more. Pour in the coconut milk and the measurement water, add the lemon grass, fish sauce and sugar and leave to simmer for 10 minutes.

Add the mussels, cover and cook for 3–5 minutes until the mussels are open, discarding any that remain closed. Scatter over the coriander to serve.

For spicy wok-roasted mussels, heat 1 tablespoon vegetable oil in a large wok, add 1 tablespoon Thai green curry paste and cook for 1 minute. Add 1 kg (2 lb) live mussels, scrubbed and debearded, and cook for 1 minute. Pour over 50 ml (2 fl oz) coconut milk, cover and cook for 2 minutes more until the mussels are open, discarding any that remain closed. Scatter over 1 chopped spring onion, a handful of chopped fresh coriander and 1 tablespoon lime juice to serve. **Total cooking time 10 minutes.**

mustard & curry leaf halibut

Serves **4**
Total cooking time **30 minutes**

1 teaspoon **ground turmeric**
1 tablespoon **chilli powder**
2 tablespoons grated **fresh coconut**
4 tablespoons **vegetable oil**
1 teaspoon **black mustard seeds**
20 **fresh curry leaves**
2 **onions**, thinly sliced
4 **green chillies**, deseeded and sliced
2.5 cm (1 inch) piece of **fresh root ginger**, peeled and cut into matchsticks
6 **garlic cloves**, finely chopped
1 kg (2¼ lb) **skinless halibut fillets**, boned and cut into bite-sized pieces
400 ml (14 fl oz) **coconut milk**
300 ml (½ pint) **water**
1 tablespoon **tamarind paste**
salt
steamed **basmati rice**, to serve (optional)

Mix together the turmeric, chilli powder and coconut in a small bowl and set aside.

Heat the oil in a large wok or heavy-based saucepan until hot, then add the mustard seeds and cook over a medium-high heat for a few minutes until the seeds begin to pop, then add the curry leaves, onions, green chillies, ginger and garlic and stir-fry for about 5 minutes until fragrant.

Stir in the turmeric mixture and stir-fry for a further 1 minute. Add the fish, then stir in the coconut milk and measurement water. Finally, add the tamarind paste. Bring to the boil, then reduce the heat to low and simmer gently, uncovered, for 15 minutes or until the fish is cooked through. Season well with salt.

Ladle into bowls and serve with steamed basmati rice, if liked.

For pan-fried fish with mustard & curry leaves,

mix together 2 tablespoons wholegrain mustard, 6 crushed dried curry leaves, 1 teaspoon chilli powder and 1 teaspoon medium or hot curry powder in a bowl. Season with salt, then spread the mixture all over 4 skinless plaice fillets. Heat 2 tablespoons sunflower oil in a large frying pan and fry the fish fillets for 2–3 minutes on each side or until cooked through. Serve with a green salad. **Total cooking time 10 minutes.**

goan fried fish

Serves **4**
Total cooking time **10 minutes**

1 teaspoon **ground turmeric**
1 teaspoon **ginger paste**
1 teaspoon **garlic paste**
1 teaspoon **chilli powder**
1 teaspoon **ground cumin**
1 teaspoon **ground coriander**
juice of 2 **lemons**
4 **skinless halibut steaks**,
    about 200 g (7 oz) each
4 tablespoons **sunflower oil**
salt and **pepper**
green salad, to serve
    (optional)

Mix together the ground spices and pastes in a bowl. Add the lemon juice and stir to mix well. Spread the mixture all over the fish and season well.

Heat the sunflower oil in a large frying pan, add the fish and fry over a medium-high heat for 2–3 minutes on each side or until just cooked through. Serve with a green salad, if liked.

For Goan fishcakes, place 400 g (13 oz) skinless halibut fillets, boned, and 400 g (13 oz) raw peeled prawns in a food processor or blender. Add 1 tablespoon Goan curry paste and blitz until smooth. Using wet hands, shape the mixture into 12 cakes. Heat 2 tablespoons sunflower oil in a large frying pan, add the fishcakes and fry over a medium-high heat for 3–4 minutes on each side or until cooked through. Serve with steamed rice and a salad. **Total cooking time 20 minutes.**

coconut spiced clams

Serves **4**
Total cooking time **20 minutes**

4 tablespoons **vegetable oil**
2 **shallots**, very finely chopped
1 **red chilli**, slit lengthways
   and deseeded
3 cm (1 inch) piece of **fresh
   root ginger**, peeled and
   shredded
2 **garlic cloves**, finely chopped
2 **plum tomatoes**, finely
   chopped
1 tablespoon **medium** or **hot
   curry powder**
200 ml (7 fl oz) **coconut milk**
800 g (1¾ lb) **fresh clams**,
   scrubbed
large handful of chopped **fresh
   coriander**
3 tablespoons grated **fresh
   coconut**

To serve (optional)
salad
crusty bread

Heat the oil in a large wok or saucepan until hot, add the shallots, red chilli, ginger and garlic and stir-fry over a medium heat for 3–4 minutes. Increase the heat to high, stir in the tomatoes, curry powder and coconut milk and cook for a further 4–5 minutes.

Add the clams to the pan, discarding any that have cracked or don't shut when tapped, stir to mix and cover tightly, then continue to cook over a high heat for 6–8 minutes until the clams have opened. Discard any that remain closed.

Stir in the chopped coriander and sprinkle over the grated coconut. Ladle into bowls and serve immediately, with a fresh salad and crusty bread to mop up the juices, if liked.

For spicy clam & coconut chowder, heat 2 tablespoons sunflower oil in a heavy-based saucepan, add 1 chopped onion, 1 deseeded and chopped red chilli, 1 tablespoon medium or hot curry powder and 2 chopped garlic cloves and cook, stirring, for 2–3 minutes. Add 400 g (13 oz) peeled and finely diced potatoes, 200 ml (7 fl oz) coconut milk and 600 ml (1 pint) hot fish stock. Bring to the boil, then reduce the heat to medium and cook, uncovered, for 12–15 minutes or until the potatoes are tender. Increase the heat to high, stir in 400 g (13 oz) fresh scrubbed clams, discarding any that are cracked or don't shut when tapped, cover tightly and bring to the boil. Cook for 4–5 minutes or until the clams have opened. Discard any that remain closed. Season, stir in a small handful of chopped fresh coriander and serve immediately. **Total cooking time 30 minutes.**

chilli seafood stew

Serves **2**
Total cooking time **30 minutes**

2 tablespoons **olive oil**
1 **red onion**, cut into slim
   wedges
1 small **red chilli**, deseeded
   and thinly sliced
1 **garlic clove**, sliced
250 g (8 oz) **potatoes**, peeled
   and cubed
200 g (7 oz) **ready-prepared**
   squid rings
150 ml (¼ pint) **water**
400 g (13 oz) can **chopped**
   tomatoes
150 ml (¼ pint) **white wine**
3 tablespoons **sun-dried**
   tomato paste
2 tablespoons chopped
   sun-blush tomatoes in oil,
   drained
2 tablespoons **thyme leaves**
250 g (8 oz) **live mussels**,
   scrubbed and debearded
175 g (6 oz) **red mullet fillets**,
   skinned and cut into chunks
crusty bread, to serve
   (optional)

Heat the oil in a large frying pan, add the onion, chilli and garlic and cook over a medium heat for 5–8 minutes until pale golden and softened. Add the potatoes and squid rings and cook for a further 2 minutes.

Pour over the measurement water, chopped tomatoes, wine and tomato paste and stir well. Add the sun-blush tomatoes and thyme and cook for 8 minutes.

Meanwhile, sort through the mussels, discarding any that don't shut when tapped.

Add the red mullet to the pan and stir gently through, then add the mussels, cover and bring to the boil. Cook for 5–7 minutes, shaking the pan occasionally until the fish is cooked through and the mussels have opened. Discard any that remain closed. Serve with warm crusty bread to mop up the juices, if liked.

For seafood, chilli & tomato pan-fry, heat 1 tablespoon olive oil in a frying pan, add 1 small roughly chopped onion and cook for 2 minutes. Add a 400 g (13 oz) can chopped tomatoes, ½ teaspoon dried chilli flakes, 150 ml (¼ pint) white wine and a 300 g (10 oz) pack seafood selection and bring to the boil. Reduce the heat, cover and simmer for 5 minutes until piping hot. Serve with crusty bread. **Total cooking time 10 minutes.**

prawn & mango curry

Serves **4**

Total cooking time **20 minutes**

2 tablespoons **vegetable oil**
2 **garlic cloves**, finely chopped
2 **shallots**, thinly sliced
1 **carrot**, peeled and cut into
  thin matchsticks
8 cm (3 inch) length of
  trimmed **lemon grass stalk**,
  finely chopped
1 **red chilli**, deseeded and
  chopped
1 tablespoon **hot curry
  powder**
300 ml (½ pint) **coconut milk**
200 ml (7 fl oz) **water**
1 tablespoon **fish sauce**
1 kg (2¼ lb) **raw king prawns**,
  peeled and deveined, with
  tails left on
300 g (10 oz) **mango** flesh,
  cut into 1.5 cm (¾ inch)
  cubes
Thai basil leaves, to garnish
steamed **jasmine rice**, to
  serve

Heat the oil in a heavy-based saucepan, add the garlic, shallots and carrot and cook over a medium heat, stirring occasionally, for 1–2 minutes until softened. Add the lemon grass, red chilli and curry powder and cook for a further 3 minutes or until fragrant.

Pour in the coconut milk, measurement water and fish sauce and bring to a simmer. Cook for 5 minutes, then reduce the heat to medium-low, stir in the prawns and mango and simmer gently, partially covered, for 5 minutes or until the prawns turn pink and are cooked through.

Ladle into bowls, scatter with Thai basil leaves and serve with steamed jasmine rice.

For prawn, lemon grass & mango stir-fry, heat 2 tablespoons sunflower oil in a large wok until hot, add 2 chopped shallots, 2 deseeded and chopped red chillies, 2 chopped garlic cloves and an 8 cm (3 inch) length of trimmed lemon grass stalk, finely chopped, and stir-fry over a high heat for 1 minute. Add 1 tablespoon hot curry powder, 600 g (1 lb 5 oz) cooked peeled prawns and the diced flesh of 1 ripe mango and stir-fry for a further 3–4 minutes or until piping hot. Serve with noodles. **Total cooking time 10 minutes.**

cajun spiced salmon frittata

Serves **4**

Total cooking time **20 minutes**

1 tablespoon **olive oil**

1 **red pepper**, cored, deseeded and cut into chunks

1 **green pepper**, cored, deseeded and cut into chunks

1 small **onion**, sliced

1 small **red chilli**, deseeded and finely chopped

6 tablespoons chopped **fresh coriander**, plus extra to garnish

250 g (8 oz) **skinless salmon fillets**

2.5 cm (1 inch) piece of **fresh root ginger**, peeled and roughly chopped

2 teaspoons **Cajun spice mix**

6 **eggs**

pepper

salad, to serve (optional)

Heat the oil in a 23 cm (9 inch) nonstick frying pan and cook the peppers, onion and chilli over a medium heat, stirring occasionally, for 3–4 minutes until beginning to soften. Stir in the coriander, then make a well in the centre of the pan, add the salmon fillets and cook for 3–4 minutes, turning once, until almost cooked through.

Flake the fillets into chunky pieces in the pan, then add the ginger and spice mix and gently toss all the ingredients together.

Beat the eggs in a jug and season with a little pepper. Pour over the vegetables and salmon and gently cook for 3–4 minutes until the base of the frittata is set.

Place the pan under a preheated medium grill, making sure that the pan handle is turned away from the heat, and cook for 4–5 minutes until the top is golden and set. Cut into wedges and serve with salad, if liked.

For simple Cajun salmon, mix a squeeze of ginger paste with 2 teaspoons Cajun spice mix and rub into the flesh of 250 g (8 oz) skinless salmon fillets. Heat 3 tablespoons olive oil in a large frying pan and cook the salmon over a medium heat for 9 minutes, turning halfway through. Serve with bread and salad. **Total cooking time 10 minutes.**

roasted garlicky herb sea bass

Serves **2**

Total cooking time **30 minutes**

2 **whole sea bass**, about
   300 g (10 oz) each, gutted
1 **garlic clove**, sliced
4 tablespoons chopped
   parsley
2 tablespoons chopped **thyme
   leaves**
1 **lemon**, halved and sliced
1 **fennel bulb**, trimmed and
   thinly sliced
375 g (12 oz) **potatoes**, cut
   into slim wedges
1 tablespoon **olive oil**
salt and **pepper**

Place the fish in a roasting tin and slash both sides deep to the bone. Season well with pepper.

Mix together the garlic and herbs in a bowl, then rub the mixture over the fish, pushing it into the slashes. Tuck the lemon slices and fennel under and around the fish.

Toss the potatoes with the oil and season well, then arrange on top of the lemon and fennel.

Roast in a preheated oven, 200°C (400°F), Gas Mark 6, for 20–25 minutes, or until the potatoes are golden and the fish is cooked through.

For pan-fried sea bass & fennel, slash 2 gutted sea bass, about 300 g (10 oz) each, several times on each side and season well. Heat 25 g (1 oz) butter in a large frying pan, add 1 small trimmed and thinly sliced fennel bulb and 1 thinly sliced garlic clove and cook over a medium heat for 3–4 minutes until slightly softened. Add the fish to the pan and cook for 4 minutes on each side, or until the flesh is opaque and cooked through. Scatter with 1 tablespoon chopped thyme leaves and season well. Serve with crusty bread. **Total cooking time 20 minutes.**

thai green curry with monkfish

Serves **4**
Total cooking time **30 minutes**

2 tablespoons **Thai green
  curry paste**
handful of chopped **fresh
  coriander**
1 tablespoon **vegetable oil**
300 ml (½ pint) **fish** or
  chicken stock
400 ml (14 fl oz) **coconut milk**
2 tablespoons **fish sauce**
2 teaspoons **soft brown sugar**
500 g (1 lb) **skinless
  monkfish fillet**, cut into
  2.5 cm (1 inch) cubes
75 g (3 oz) **cherry tomatoes**,
  halved
handful of chopped **basil**, to
  garnish

Put the Thai green curry paste and coriander in a mini
food processor and whizz to a smooth paste.

Heat the oil in a large saucepan. Add the curry paste
and stir around the pan for 3–5 minutes until the oil
starts to separate. Pour over the stock and coconut milk
and bring to the boil. Add the fish sauce and sugar and
leave to simmer for 10 minutes.

Stir in the monkfish and tomatoes and cook for a
further 7–10 minutes until just cooked through. Scatter
over the basil and serve.

For monkfish & bean curry, heat 2 tablespoons
vegetable oil in a large saucepan. Add 2 tablespoons
Thai green curry paste and cook for 3 minutes until
the oil starts to separate. Pour over 300 ml (½ pint)
fish or chicken stock, 400 ml (14 fl oz) coconut milk,
2 tablespoons fish sauce and 2 teaspoons soft brown
sugar. Simmer for 10 minutes. Add 150 g (5 oz) green
beans and cook for 1–2 minutes. Stir in 500 g (1 lb)
skinless monkfish fillet, cut into 2.5 cm (1 inch) cubes,
and cook for 3–5 minutes. Scatter over a handful of
basil leaves to serve. **Total cooking time 20 minutes.**

chilli cod in tomato sauce

Serves **4**
Total cooking time **30 minutes**

2 tablespoons **olive oil**
1 **onion**, diced
2 **garlic cloves**, crushed
¼ teaspoon **dried chilli flakes**
1 **red pepper**, cored,
    deseeded and thinly sliced
400 g (13 oz) can **chopped
    tomatoes**
100 ml (3½ fl oz) **white wine**
12 **black olives**, pitted and
    sliced
4 **skinless cod loin fillets**,
    about 150 g (5 oz) each
steamed **green beans**, to
    serve (optional)

Heat the olive oil in a large frying pan and sauté the onion, garlic and chilli flakes for 3–4 minutes. Add the red pepper and cook for a further 3–4 minutes.

Pour in the chopped tomatoes, white wine and black olives and simmer for 8 minutes.

Add the cod loin fillets to the pan and cook for 8–10 minutes, turning once if not covered by the liquid, until cooked through. Serve with steamed green beans, if liked.

For pesto-crusted cod, heat 1 tablespoon olive oil in a flameproof frying pan and cook 4 x 150 g (5 oz) cod fillets for 2–3 minutes. Mix together 4 tablespoons fresh breadcrumbs with ½ red chilli, deseeded and finely diced, 2 tablespoons ready-made pesto and 3 sliced spring onions. Spoon the breadcrumb mixture over the fish and press down lightly. Sprinkle with 1 tablespoon grated Parmesan cheese and cook under a preheated hot grill for 2–3 minutes, until golden and cooked through. Serve with a crisp green salad. **Total cooking time 10 minutes.**

scallop, bacon & pine nut pan-fry

Serves **4**
Total cooking time **10 minutes**

25 g (1 oz) **butter**
300 g (10 oz) **smoked
  streaky bacon**, cut into
  pieces
350 g (11½ oz) **scallops**,
  halved widthways if large
4 tablespoons **pine nuts**
8 tablespoons chopped
  parsley
finely grated rind of 1 **lemon**
crusty bread, to serve

Heat the butter in a large frying pan, add the bacon and cook over a high heat for 3 minutes until golden.

Add the scallops and pine nuts and cook for 3–4 minutes until the scallops are cooked through and the pine nuts are golden. Stir in the parsley and lemon rind. Divide the mixture between 4 dishes, spoon over any juices and serve with plenty of crusty bread.

For griddled scallops in bacon, place 16 large scallops, 2 tablespoons chopped parsley and the finely grated rind of 1 lemon in a bowl and toss well to coat. Wrap 1 streaky bacon rasher around each scallop, then secure with cocktail sticks. Heat 25 g (1 oz) butter in a griddle pan, add the scallops and cook over a high heat for 2 minutes on each side until golden and cooked through. Serve with salad and crusty bread. **Total cooking time 20 minutes.**

cod, red mullet & prawn stew

Serves **4**

Total cooking time **20 minutes**

1 tablespoon **olive oil**

1 **fennel bulb**, quartered and thinly sliced

2 **garlic cloves**, thinly sliced

400 g (13 oz) can **chopped tomatoes**

pinch of **saffron threads**

900 ml (1½ pints) hot **fish stock**

250 g (8 oz) **cod loin**, cut into bite-sized pieces

200 g (7 oz) **cooked peeled king prawns**

2 **red mullet fillets**, halved lengthways

50 g (2 oz) **spinach leaves**

crusty wholemeal bread, to serve

Heat the oil in a large frying pan, add the fennel and garlic and cook for 4–5 minutes until softened. Stir in the tomatoes and saffron, then pour in the stock and bring to a simmer.

Add the cod, prawns and red mullet and simmer for 6–8 minutes or until the fish is cooked through.

Stir in the spinach until wilted, then serve immediately with crusty wholemeal bread.

For quick cod, red mullet & prawn curry, heat 1 tablespoon oil in a large frying pan or wok, add 1 chopped onion and 2 chopped garlic cloves and sauté for 1 minute. Stir in 2 tablespoons curry paste and 400 ml (14 fl oz) coconut milk and bring to a simmer. Add 200 g (7 oz) cod loin and 2 red mullet fillets, each cut into bite-sized pieces, and 250 g (8 oz) cooked peeled king prawns. Simmer for 6–8 minutes until the fish is cooked through. Stir in 125 g (4 oz) spinach leaves and 2 tablespoons roughly chopped coriander. Season and serve with rice. **Total cooking time 10 minutes.**

quick fish stew with chickpeas

Serves **4**
Total cooking time **20 minutes**

2 tablespoons **olive oil**
1 **celery stick**, thinly sliced
2 **garlic cloves**, chopped
1 teaspoon **sweet paprika**
125 ml (4 fl oz) **dry white
    wine**
400 g (13 oz) can **good-
    quality ratatouille**
400 g (13 oz) can **chickpeas,**
    rinsed and drained
1 teaspoon grated **lemon** rind
75 ml (3 fl oz) **vegetable
    stock**
400 g (13 oz) **boneless fish
    fillets**, such as haddock, cod
    or salmon, cut into bite-sized
    pieces
salt and **pepper**
chopped **parsley**, to garnish
wholegrain rice or **couscous,**
    to serve

Heat the oil in a large saucepan and cook the celery and garlic over a medium heat for 3–4 minutes, to soften.

Add the paprika, stir for 1 minute, then pour in the wine and simmer to reduce by half.

Tip in the ratatouille along with the chickpeas, lemon rind and stock, then season to taste and simmer for 5–6 minutes, to thicken slightly.

Stir the fish into the stew, cover and simmer for a further 3–5 minutes, or until the fish is cooked and flaky. Garnish with chopped parsley and serve with rice or couscous.

For baked fish with chickpeas, prepare the stew following the recipe above, adding 1 small diced head of fennel to the celery and garlic and cooking for 5–6 minutes before adding the paprika. Once the stew has simmered for 5–6 minutes, transfer it to an ovenproof dish and place 4 skinless, boneless fish fillets on top. Drizzle with 1 tablespoon olive oil, season and bake, uncovered, in a preheated oven, 200°C (400°F), Gas Mark 6, for 12–15 minutes. Serve with rice or couscous and garnished with chopped parsley. **Total cooking time 30 minutes.**

spicy prawn & pea pilau

Serves **4**
Total cooking time **30 minutes**

1 tablespoon **sunflower oil**
1 tablespoon **butter**
1 **large onion**, finely chopped
2 **garlic cloves**, finely chopped
1 tablespoon **medium** or **hot curry paste**
250 g (8 oz) **basmati rice**
600 ml (1 pint) hot **fish** or **vegetable stock**
300 g (10 oz) **frozen peas**
finely grated rind and juice of 1 large **lime**
20 g (¾ oz) **fresh coriander**, finely chopped
400 g (13 oz) **cooked peeled prawns**
salt and **pepper**

Heat the oil and butter in a heavy-based saucepan, add the onion and cook over a medium heat for 2–3 minutes until softened. Stir in the garlic and curry paste and cook for a further 1–2 minutes until fragrant, then add the rice and stir to coat well.

Stir in the stock, peas and lime rind, then season well and bring to the boil. Cover tightly, then reduce the heat to low and cook for 12–15 minutes or until the liquid is absorbed and the rice is tender.

Remove the pan from the heat, then stir in the lime juice, coriander and prawns. Cover and leave the prawns to heat through for a few minutes before serving.

For spicy prawn & pea stir-fried rice, heat 2 tablespoons sunflower oil in a large wok or frying pan until hot, add 1 tablespoon medium curry paste, 400 g (12 oz) cooked peeled prawns, 200 g (7 oz) frozen peas and 500 g (1 lb) ready-cooked basmati rice and stir-fry over a high heat for 4–5 minutes or until piping hot. Remove from the heat, season and stir in 6 tablespoons chopped fresh coriander. Serve immediately. **Total cooking time 10 minutes.**

vegetarian

spiced coconut squash soup

Serves **4–6**

Total cooking time **20 minutes**

2 tablespoons **oil**
1 **onion**, chopped
2 teaspoons finely chopped
  fresh root ginger
½ teaspoon **ground coriander**
1 **lemon grass stalk**
1 strip of **orange** peel
1 kg (2 lb) **butternut squash**,
  peeled and chopped
1 litre (1¾ pints) **vegetable
  stock**
125 ml (4 fl oz) **coconut milk**
salt and **pepper**

To serve
1 **red chilli**, deseeded and
  chopped
handful of chopped **fresh
  coriander**

Heat the oil in a large saucepan, add the onion and cook for 5 minutes until softened. Add the ginger, ground coriander, lemon grass, orange peel and squash. Pour in the stock and coconut milk and bring to the boil. Leave to simmer for 12–15 minutes until the squash is soft.

Remove the lemon grass and orange peel and use a stick blender to blend the soup until smooth. Season to taste and divide between serving bowls. Sprinkle over the chilli and fresh coriander to serve.

For coconut squash rice pot, heat 2 tablespoons oil in a large saucepan, add 1 chopped onion and cook for 5 minutes until softened. Stir in 1 crushed garlic clove and 1 teaspoon finely chopped fresh root ginger, followed by 2 tablespoons Thai red curry paste. Add ½ peeled and chopped butternut squash and cook for a couple of minutes until well coated. Stir through 300 g (10 oz) jasmine rice. Pour over 500 ml (17 fl oz) vegetable stock and 125 ml (4 fl oz) coconut milk. Bring to the boil and cook for 10 minutes, then reduce the heat and simmer gently for 5 minutes until the rice and squash are just cooked through. Scatter over a handful of chopped fresh coriander leaves before serving. **Total cooking time 30 minutes.**

quick garlicky tomato lentils

Serves **4**

Total cooking time **10 minutes**

2 tablespoons **olive** or
   vegetable oil

1 large **onion**, chopped

2 **garlic cloves**, chopped

440 g (14¼ oz) jar **tomato-
   based pasta sauce**

1 teaspoon **dried oregano** or
   mixed herbs (optional)

2 x 390 g (12½ oz) cans
   green lentils, rinsed and
   drained

100 g (3½ oz) grated
   **Cheddar cheese, Parmesan
   cheese** or **other hard Italian
   cheese** (optional)

crusty bread, to serve

Heat the oil in a large frying pan and cook the onion and garlic over a medium heat for 6–7 minutes, stirring frequently, until softened. Add the pasta sauce, dried oregano or mixed herbs, if using, and lentils and heat to simmering point.

Spoon into bowls. Scatter with grated cheese, if using, and serve immediately with crusty bread.

For garlicky tomato rice, heat 2 tablespoons olive or vegetable oil in a large saucepan and cook 1 large chopped onion and 1 cored, deseeded and chopped red, green or yellow pepper for 6–7 minutes until they begin to soften. Add 2 chopped garlic cloves and cook for a further minute, then stir in 250 g (8oz) long-grain white rice. Add 2 x 400 g (13 oz) cans chopped tomatoes, 1 teaspoon dried oregano or mixed herbs, 450 ml (¾ pint) boiling water and 1 crumbled vegetable stock cube. Stir well to combine, then reduce the heat, cover with a lid and simmer gently for 18–20 minutes until the rice is tender and most of the liquid has been absorbed. Spoon into bowls and serve with a hot chilli sauce. **Total cooking time 30 minutes.**

spinach & potato tortilla

Serves **4**
Total cooking time **20 minutes**

3 tablespoons **olive oil**
2 **onions**, finely chopped
250 g (8 oz) **cooked
    potatoes**, peeled and cut
    into 1 cm (½ in) cubes
2 **garlic cloves**, finely chopped
200 g (7 oz) **cooked spinach**,
    drained thoroughly and
    roughly chopped
4 tablespoons drained and
    finely chopped **roasted red
    pepper**, from a jar
5 **eggs**, lightly beaten
3–4 tablespoons grated
    Manchego cheese
salt and **pepper**

Heat the oil in a nonstick frying pan and add the onions and potatoes. Cook gently over a medium heat for 3–4 minutes or until the vegetables have softened but not coloured, turning and stirring often.

Add the garlic, spinach and peppers and stir to mix well.

Season the beaten eggs and pour into the frying pan, shaking the pan so that the egg is evenly spread. Cook gently for 8–10 minutes or until the base of the tortilla is set.

Sprinkle over the grated Manchego. Place the frying pan under a preheated medium-hot grill and cook for 3–4 minutes or until the top is set and golden.

Remove from the heat, cut into bite-sized squares or triangles and serve warm or at room temperature.

For spinach & potato sauté, heat 1 tablespoon vegetable oil in a large frying pan. Add 2 chopped garlic cloves, 1 finely chopped onion and 1 tablespoon curry powder. Stir in 100 ml (3½ fl oz) passata, 300 g (10 oz) baby leaf spinach and 200 g (7 oz) cooked, cubed potatoes. Sauté over a high heat for 2–3 minutes or until piping hot. Season and serve with crusty bread or rice. **Total cooking time 10 minutes.**

coconut soup with squash

Serves **4**
Total cooking time **20 minutes**

1 tablespoon **vegetable oil**
1 **onion**, finely chopped
500 g (1 lb) **butternut
squash**, peeled, deseeded
and cut into cubes
1 small **red chilli**, deseeded
and finely chopped
1 teaspoon **ground coriander**
400 ml (14 fl oz) **coconut milk**
600 ml (1 pint) **vegetable
stock**
300 g (10 oz) **spinach leaves**
warm **naan breads**, to serve

Heat the oil in a large, heavy-based saucepan and cook the onion, butternut squash and chilli over a medium-high heat, stirring frequently, for 8 minutes until softened. Add the coriander and cook, stirring, for a few seconds, then stir in the coconut milk and stock and bring to the boil. Reduce the heat and simmer for 10 minutes.

Stir in the spinach leaves and cook for 1 minute until just wilted. Ladle the soup into serving bowls and serve with warm naan breads.

For quick Caribbean-style coconut soup, heat 1 tablespoon vegetable oil in a large, heavy-based saucepan and cook 1 finely chopped red onion over a medium-high heat, stirring frequently, for 3 minutes. Add 1 teaspoon ground coriander and ½ teaspoon smoked paprika and cook, stirring, for a few seconds. Stir in 400 ml (14 fl oz) coconut milk and 600 ml (1 pint) vegetable stock and bring to the boil. Add a 400 g (13 oz) can kidney beans, rinsed and drained, with 300 g (10 oz) spinach leaves and simmer for 5 minutes. Serve with corn bread. **Total cooking time 10 minutes.**

quick pea & leek soup

Serves **4**
Total cooking time **10 minutes**

50 g (2 oz) **butter**
2 **banana shallots**, finely
   chopped
2 **leeks**, very thinly sliced
1 tablespoon chopped **mixed
   herbs**, such as sage, thyme,
   chives and parsley
100 ml (3½ fl oz) **crème
   fraîche**
1 litre (1¾ pints) good-quality
   boiling **vegetable stock**
350 g (11½ oz) **frozen petit
   pois**
salt and **pepper**

Melt the butter in a large saucepan over a medium heat, then add the shallots and leeks and cook for 5–6 minutes, until softened.

Meanwhile, stir the chopped herbs into the crème fraîche and set aside.

Add the vegetable stock and petit pois to the leeks and simmer for 2–3 minutes, until the peas are just tender.

Season to taste, then ladle into bowls and serve immediately with a dollop of herby crème fraîche.

For potato, pea & leek soup, heat 2 tablespoons olive oil in a large saucepan or flameproof casserole dish and add 875 g (1¾ lb) diced potatoes, 2 chopped leeks and 3 thinly sliced spring onions. Cook over a medium heat for 5 minutes, stirring frequently, until the leek is beginning to soften. Add 1.2 litres (2 pints) boiling vegetable stock, season and simmer over a medium heat for about 12 minutes, until the potato is tender, adding 150 g (5 oz) frozen peas for the final 2–3 minutes. Blend the soup until smooth, then ladle into bowls and serve with herby crème fraîche, as above. **Total cooking time 20 minutes.**

quick carrot & coriander tagine

Serves **4**
Total cooking time **20 minutes**

2 tablespoons **olive oil**
875 g (1¾ lb) **carrots**, peeled
    and sliced
2.5 cm (1 inch) piece of **fresh
    root ginger**, peeled and
    finely chopped
2 **garlic cloves**, sliced
2 teaspoons **baharat** or **ras
    el hanout**
1 teaspoon **ground coriander**
pinch of **saffron threads**
    (optional)
8 **ready-to-eat dried apricots**,
    sliced
1 **preserved lemon**, chopped
400 ml (14 fl oz) hot
    vegetable stock
handful of chopped **fresh
    coriander**, to garnish
steamed **giant couscous**,
    to serve

Heat the oil in a large saucepan or flameproof casserole dish and cook the carrots, ginger and garlic for 5–6 minutes, until beginning to soften. Add the spices and apricots and stir for a minute before adding the preserved lemon and hot stock. Cover and simmer for 10–12 minutes, until tender.

Ladle the tagine into bowls, sprinkle with the coriander and serve with giant couscous.

For Moroccan-style carrot & coriander soup, heat 2 tablespoons olive oil in a large saucepan or flameproof casserole dish and add 1 chopped onion, 1 tablespoon peeled and chopped fresh root ginger and 2 chopped garlic cloves. Cook over a medium heat for 7–8 minutes, until softened. Stir in 1 teaspoon ras el hanout and 1 teaspoon ground coriander, then add 750 g (1½ lb) peeled and chopped carrots and 1 peeled and chopped sweet potato. Stir to coat, then pour in 1.2 litres (2 pints) hot vegetable stock. Cover and simmer over a medium heat for about 15 minutes, until the vegetables are tender. Blend the soup with a hand-held blender, then season to taste and ladle into bowls. Garnish with plenty of chopped fresh coriander to serve. **Total cooking time 30 minutes.**

pan-cooked eggs

Serves **2**
Total cooking time **10 minutes**

25 g (1 oz) **butter**
1 **leek**, thinly sliced
¼ teaspoon **dried chilli flakes**
300 g (10 oz) **baby spinach leaves**
2 **eggs**
3 tablespoons **natural yogurt**
pinch of **ground paprika**
salt and **pepper**

Heat the butter in a frying pan, add the leek and chilli flakes and cook over a medium-high heat for 4–5 minutes until softened. Add the spinach and season well, then toss and cook for 2 minutes until wilted.

Make 2 wells in the vegetables and break an egg into each well. Cook over a low heat for 2–3 minutes until the eggs are set. Spoon the yogurt on top and sprinkle with the paprika.

For leek & spinach omelette, heat 1 tablespoon olive oil in a large frying pan, add 1 small leek, very thinly sliced, and cook over a medium heat for 3–4 minutes, then add 175 g (6 oz) baby spinach leaves and cook for 2 minutes, stirring, until wilted. In a jug, beat together 4 eggs and season well, then pour over the spinach mixture. Cook over a low heat for 2–3 minutes until the base is set, then place a baking sheet over the top of the pan and cook for a further 1 minute until the top is set. Gently flip one side of the omelette over on to the other, then cut the omelette in half. Lightly toast 2 pieces of walnut bread and spread each with 1 tablespoon tomato chutney, then place an omelette half over each. **Total cooking time 20 minutes.**

red pepper & spinach stew

Serves **4**

Total cooking time **20 minutes**

3 tablespoons **olive** or
vegetable oil

2 large **red peppers**, cored,
deseeded and cut into large
pieces

3 **garlic cloves**, sliced

2 teaspoons **ground cumin** or
Mexican spice mix, such as
fajita seasoning (optional)

2 tablespoons **tomato purée**

400 ml (14 fl oz) hot
vegetable stock

400 g (13 oz) can **chopped
tomatoes**

610 g (1 lb 3¾ oz) **canned
kidney beans**, rinsed and
drained

200 g (7 oz) **frozen leaf
spinach**, defrosted and
drained

salt and **pepper**

Heat the oil in a saucepan and cook the peppers and garlic over a medium heat for 5–6 minutes, stirring frequently, until softened.

Stir in the cumin, if using, and cook for 1 minute before adding the tomato purée, hot stock, chopped tomatoes and kidney beans. Bring to the boil, season to taste, then cover and simmer gently for 10–12 minutes until thickened slightly. Stir in the spinach for the final minute of cooking, then ladle into bowls to serve.

For red pepper & kidney bean soup, cook the peppers and garlic as above until softened. Add the ground cumin and cook for a minute, then pour in 750 ml (1¼ pints) hot vegetable stock, 500 g (1 lb) sieved tomatoes or passata and 2 x 400 g (13 oz) cans kidney beans, rinsed and drained, reserving about 200 g (7 oz) of the beans. Season to taste, then cover, bring to a boil and simmer for about 15 minutes until slightly thickened. Use a stick blender to blend the soup, then stir through the reserved beans, 150 g (5 oz) defrosted chopped spinach and heat through. Ladle into bowls to serve, scattered with chopped parsley. **Total cooking time 30 minutes.**

quick mushroom & garlic tom yum

Serves **4**

Total cooking time **10 minutes**

1 tablespoon **tom yum paste**
1 litre (1¾ pints) **vegetable stock**
150 g (5 oz) **oyster mushrooms**, sliced
200 g (7 oz) **closed-cup mushrooms**, sliced
100 g (3½ oz) **enoki mushrooms** (optional)
2 **spring onions**, thinly sliced
2 **garlic cloves**, sliced
2.5 cm (1 inch) piece **fresh root ginger**, peeled and sliced
lime juice, to serve

Place the tom yum paste in a large saucepan with the stock and bring to a simmer. Add the mushrooms, spring onions, garlic and ginger and simmer for 5–6 minutes, so the flavours develop and the mushrooms soften.

Ladle into bowls and serve immediately with a squeeze of lime juice.

For wild mushroom & garlic broth, place 25 g (1 oz) mixed dried mushrooms in a pan with 1 litre (1¾ pints) just simmering water. Cover and cook for 10 minutes, until softened. Meanwhile, heat 2 tablespoons oil in a saucepan and cook 1 diced celery stick, 1 sliced leek, 2 chopped shallots and 2 chopped garlic cloves for 7–8 minutes over a medium heat until softened. Add 300 g (10 oz) sliced portobello mushrooms and cook for a further 2 minutes, until just beginning to soften. Strain the dried mushrooms, reserving the liquid, then slice and add to the vegetables. Stir, then add the reserved mushroom stock and simmer for 4–5 minutes. Ladle into bowls and serve. **Total cooking time 20 minutes.**

red cabbage & beetroot lentils

Serves **2**
Total cooking time **20 minutes**

2 tablespoons **olive or vegetable oil**
½ small **red cabbage**, thinly sliced
2 **spring onions**, sliced, plus extra to garnish
1 **beetroot**, coarsely grated
1 teaspoon **ground cumin**
300 g (10 oz) **canned green lentils**, rinsed and drained
salt and **pepper**
natural or **Greek yogurt**, to serve

Heat the oil in a saucepan and cook the red cabbage and spring onion over a medium heat for about 5 minutes until just beginning to soften. Stir in the beetroot, then cover and cook for a further 8–10 minutes, stirring occasionally, until the vegetables are tender.

Sprinkle over the ground cumin and stir over the heat for a minute, then add the lentils and warm through. Season to taste, then spoon into 2 dishes and serve with a dollop of yogurt and extra sliced spring onions.

For fruity braised red cabbage, heat 2 tablespoons olive or vegetable oil in a saucepan and gently cook 1 finely chopped red onion over a medium heat for 6–7 minutes until softened. Add 1 chopped garlic clove and 1 teaspoon ground cumin, then stir in ½ shredded red cabbage, 1 peeled and coarsely grated dessert apple and a small handful of raisins. Cook gently for about 15 minutes, stirring frequently, until the vegetables are softened but still have some bite. Season to taste, then stir in 2 teaspoons balsamic vinegar and serve with grilled vegetarian sausages. **Total cooking time 30 minutes.**

black-eyed bean stew

Total cooking time **30 minutes**

2 tablespoons **olive oil**

4 **shallots**, finely chopped

2 **garlic cloves**, crushed

2 **celery stalks**, diced

1 large **carrot**, peeled and cut
   into 1 cm (½ in) pieces

1 **red pepper**, cored,
   deseeded and cut into
   1 cm (½ in) pieces

1 teaspoon **dried mixed
   herbs**

2 teaspoons **ground cumin**

1 teaspoon **ground cinnamon**

2 x 400 g (13 oz) cans
   tomatoes

2 tablespoons **sun-dried
   tomato purée**

75 ml (3 fl oz) **vegetable
   stock**

2 x 400 g (13 oz) cans **black-
   eyed beans in water**, rinsed
   and drained

4 tablespoons finely chopped
   fresh coriander, plus extra
   leaves to garnish

salt and **pepper**

basmati rice, to serve

Heat the oil in a large frying pan and place over a
high heat.

Add the shallots, garlic, celery, carrot and red pepper
and stir-fry for 2–3 minutes or until lightly starting
to brown.

Sprinkle in the dried herbs, cumin and cinnamon, add
the tomatoes, purée and stock and bring to the boil.
Reduce the heat to medium, cover and cook gently
for 12–15 minutes or until the vegetables are tender,
breaking up the tomatoes into small pieces with a
wooden spoon towards the end of the cooking time.

Stir in the black-eyed beans and cook for 2–3 minutes
or until piping hot.

Season well, remove from the heat and sprinkle over
the chopped coriander. Garnish with coriander leaves
and serve with basmati rice.

For hearty bean & vegetable broth, place 1 peeled
and finely diced carrot, 2 finely diced celery stalks,
2 finely diced shallots, 2 crushed garlic cloves,
2 tablespoons sun-dried tomato purée and 2 teaspoons
dried mixed herbs in a heavy-based saucepan with
1 litre (1¾ pints) hot vegetable stock and bring to the
boil. Cook, uncovered, over a medium heat for 10–12
minutes. Stir in 2 x 400 g (13 oz) cans black-eyed beans,
rinsed and drained, and bring back to the boil. Season,
remove from the heat and serve ladled into bowls with
crusty bread. **Total cooking time 20 minutes.**

savoy cabbage & parmesan soup

Serves **4**

Total cooking time **30 minutes**

4 tablespoons **olive oil**

1 **onion**, chopped

2 **garlic cloves**, crushed

½ teaspoon **fennel seeds**

1 **Savoy cabbage**

1 **potato**, peeled and diced

1 litre (1¾ pints) **vegetable stock**

75 g (3 oz) grated **Parmesan cheese**, plus extra

1 tablespoon to serve

salt and **pepper**

crusty bread, to serve

Heat 2 tablespoons of the olive oil in a saucepan and sauté the onion, garlic and fennel seeds for 3–4 minutes.

Shred 4 leaves of the cabbage and reserve. Finely shred the remaining cabbage, add to the pan with the diced potato and cook for 3–4 minutes, then pour in the stock.

Simmer for 10 minutes, until the potato is tender. Stir in the grated Parmesan.

Blend with a stick blender, or in a food processor, until smooth. Season to taste.

Heat the remaining olive oil and stir-fry the reserved cabbage. Top each bowl of soup with the fried cabbage.

Serve sprinkled with extra grated Parmesan, and slices of crusty bread on the side.

For rice with Savoy cabbage, heat 3 tablespoons olive oil in a frying pan and sauté 1 chopped onion for 2–3 minutes. Stir in 450 g (14½ oz) finely shredded Savoy cabbage and cook, stirring, until wilted. Stir in 250 g (8 oz) Arborio rice and 1 litre (1¾ pints) vegetable stock. Bring to the boil and simmer for 15–16 minutes, until the rice is al dente. Stir in 25 g (1 oz) butter and 40 g (1¾ oz) grated Parmesan, season and serve. **Total cooking time 20 minutes.**

bean & vegetable nut crumble

Serves **4**
Total cooking time **30 minutes**

75 g (3 oz) **butter**, chilled and
    diced
175 g (6 oz) **plain flour**
100 g (3½ oz) **walnuts**,
    chopped
50 g (2 oz) **Cheddar cheese**,
    grated
2 x 250 g (8 oz) packs
    **prepared broccoli,
    cauliflower** and **carrots**
500 g (1 lb) jar **ready-made
    tomato and herb sauce**
2 **garlic cloves**, crushed
6 tablespoons finely chopped
    basil leaves
400 g (13 oz) can **butter
    beans**, rinsed and drained
salt and **pepper**

Rub the butter into the plain flour until crumbs form.
Stir in the chopped walnuts and grated cheese, season
and set aside.

Remove the carrots from the packs of prepared
vegetables, roughly chop and boil in a large saucepan
for 2 minutes. Add the broccoli and cauliflower and
cook for another minute, then drain.

Pour the tomato and herb sauce over the blanched
vegetables and heat until bubbling.

Stir in the garlic, basil and butter beans. Transfer to
a medium-sized ovenproof dish and scatter over the
crumble mixture. Bake in a preheated oven, 200°C
(400°F), Gas Mark 6, for 15–20 minutes or until golden
and bubbling.

For butter bean and walnut pâté, tip 2 x 400 g
(13 oz) cans butter beans, rinsed and drained, and
the juice and finely grated zest of 1 lemon into a food
processor with 1 crushed garlic clove, 4 tablespoons
each of finely chopped basil and mint leaves, 50 g
(2 oz) chopped walnuts, 8 tablespoons ready-made
mayonnaise and 2 teaspoons Dijon mustard. Blend
until fairly smooth and serve spread thickly on toasted
sourdough bread with a salad. **Total cooking time
10 minutes.**

malaysian stew

Serves **4**
Total cooking time **30 minutes**

2 tablespoons **vegetable oil**
1 **medium onion**, thinly sliced
6 tablespoons **laksa curry paste**
2 x 400 ml (14 fl oz) cans **coconut milk**
300 ml (½ pint) **water**
1 teaspoon **salt**
200 g (7 oz) peeled **potatoes**, cut into 1.5 cm (¾ in) pieces
250 g (8 oz) peeled **carrots**, cut into 1.5 cm (¾ in) pieces
100 g (3½ oz) **fine green beans**, topped, tailed and halved
150 g (5 oz) **cauliflower florets**
300 g (10 oz) peeled and deseeded **butternut squash**, cut into 1.5 cm (¾ in) pieces
50 g (2 oz) **cashew nuts**
50 g (2 oz) **beansprouts**
4 **spring onions**, trimmed and sliced on the diagonal
handful of **Thai sweet basil leaves** or **fresh coriander**

Heat the oil in a large pan over a medium heat. Add the onion and the curry paste and fry gently for 2–3 minutes until it begins to smell fragrant.

Pour in the coconut milk and measurement water, add the salt and bring to the boil.

Add the potatoes and carrots and cook for 10 minutes, then add the green beans, cauliflower and squash and cook for a further 7 minutes.

Sprinkle over the cashew nuts and simmer for 3 minutes until the vegetables are just tender.

Stir in the beansprouts, spring onions and basil or coriander. Simmer for 1 minute and serve immediately.

For quick Asian coconut soup, heat 1 tablespoon vegetable oil in a large wok and add 6 chopped spring onions, 1 tablespoon laksa curry paste, 400 ml (14 fl oz) coconut milk, 400 ml (14 fl oz) vegetable stock and 300 g (10 oz) pack stir-fry vegetables. Bring to the boil and cook over a high heat for 4–5 minutes. Season and serve. **Total cooking time 10 minutes.**

southern-style rice

Serves **4**
Total cooking time **30 minutes**

1 ½ tablespoons **vegetable oil**
1 large **onion**, chopped
2 **garlic cloves**, roughly
    chopped
1 **celery stick**, chopped
1 **red** and 1 **yellow pepper**,
    cored, deseeded and
    chopped
1 **courgette**, chopped
1 teaspoon each **dried thyme**,
    dried oregano, **hot smoked**
    paprika
¼ teaspoon **cayenne pepper**
250 g (8 oz) **long-grain rice**,
    rinsed
2 tablespoons **tomato purée**
2 x 400 g (13 oz) cans
    chopped tomatoes
450 ml (¾ pint) **vegetable**
    stock
salt and **pepper**
2 tablespoons chopped
    parsley, to garnish
few dashes **Tabasco sauce**, to
    serve (optional)

Heat the oil in a large, heavy-based casserole over a medium heat. Add the onion, garlic, celery and red and yellow peppers and cook for 4–5 minutes, stirring frequently, then add the courgette and cook for a further 3–4 minutes.

Add the herbs, spices and rice and stir-fry for 1 minute, coating the rice well in the other ingredients. Stir in the tomato purée, chopped tomatoes and vegetable stock and season. Bring to the boil and cover with a tight fitting lid, then reduce the heat and leave to simmer gently for 15–18 minutes until the rice is cooked and the mixture thickened.

Serve sprinkled with chopped parsley and a few dashes of Tabasco sauce, if liked.

For Southern-style mixed vegetable & bean stir-fry,

chop 1 large onion, 1 celery stick and 1 courgette. Core, deseed and chop 1 red and 1 yellow pepper and finely chop 2 garlic cloves. Roughly chop 2 tablespoons pickled red jalapeño peppers and set aside. Heat 1 ½ tablespoons vegetable oil in a large frying pan or wok over a medium heat, then add the raw vegetables and stir-fry for 10 minutes until tender. Add 1 teaspoon each of dried thyme, dried oregano and hot smoked paprika and ¼ teaspoon cayenne pepper and stir-fry for a further minute. Stir in 250 g (8 oz) ready-cooked plain, mushroom or chilli and bean rice, then add a 400 g (13 oz) can kidney beans, rinsed and drained. Continue to stir-fry until hot, then serve immediately in bowls, each topped with a dollop of soured cream and a scattering of chopped pickled red jalapeño peppers. **Total cooking time 20 minutes.**

tomato, rosemary & bean stew

Serves **4**
Total cooking time **10 minutes**

3 tablespoons **olive oil**
1 large **red onion**, sliced
2 teaspoons **garlic purée**
2 tablespoons chopped
   rosemary leaves
2 x 400 g (13 oz) cans
   cannellini beans, rinsed and
   drained
500 g (1 lb) jar **tomato pasta
   sauce**
wholemeal crusty bread, to
   serve

Heat the oil in a large, heavy-based frying pan and cook the onion over a medium heat, stirring occasionally, for 2 minutes. Add the garlic purée and rosemary and cook, stirring constantly, for 30 seconds.

Add the beans and tomato sauce and bring to the boil. Reduce the heat, cover and simmer for 6–7 minutes until piping hot.

Serve with fresh wholemeal bread for mopping up the juices.

For haricot bean cassoulet, heat 3 tablespoons olive oil in a large, heavy-based frying pan and cook 1 small chopped onion, 2 peeled and diced carrots and 1 tablespoon chopped rosemary leaves over a medium heat, stirring occasionally, for 3–4 minutes until softened. Add 2 x 400 g (13 oz) cans haricot beans, rinsed and drained, with 600 ml (1 pint) vegetable stock and bring to the boil. Simmer briskly, uncovered, for 10 minutes until piping hot, then place a third of the beans into a food processor and whizz until smooth. Return the puréed beans to the pan, stir to combine and heat through. Season to taste, then serve with crusty bread. **Total cooking time 20 minutes.**

spicy mushroom & cauliflower

Serves **4**
Total cooking time **30 minutes**

2 tablespoons **sunflower oil**
8 **spring onions**, cut into
    5 cm (2 inch) lengths
2 teaspoons **grated garlic**
2 teaspoons **ground ginger**
2 tablespoons **hot curry
    powder**
200 g (7 oz) **baby button
    mushrooms**
300 g (10 oz) **cauliflower
    florets**
2 **red peppers**, cored,
    deseeded and cut into
    chunks
400 g (13 oz) can **chopped
    tomatoes**
220 g (7½ oz) can **chickpeas**,
    rinsed and drained
salt and **pepper**
large handful of chopped **mint
    leaves**, to garnish
warm **naan bread**, to serve

Heat the oil in a large frying pan, add the spring onions and fry over a medium heat for 1–2 minutes. Add the garlic, ground ginger and curry powder and fry, stirring, for 20–30 seconds until fragrant, then stir in the mushrooms, cauliflower and red peppers and fry for a further 2–3 minutes.

Stir in the tomatoes and bring to the boil. Cover, then reduce the heat to medium and simmer, uncovered, for 10–15 minutes, stirring occasionally. Add the chickpeas, season and bring back to the boil.

Scatter with chopped mint and serve with warm naan.

For spicy mushroom, cauliflower & chickpea rice, heat 2 tablespoons sunflower oil in a large wok or frying pan until hot, add 1 chopped onion, 1 deseeded and chopped red chilli, 100 g (3½ oz) button mushrooms, 1 tablespoon curry powder, 100 g (3½ oz) small cauliflower florets, 100 g (3½ oz) canned chickpeas, rinsed and drained, 1 teaspoon ginger paste and 1 teaspoon garlic paste and stir-fry over a high heat for 6–8 minutes. Add 500 g (1 lb) ready-cooked basmati or long-grain rice and stir-fry for a further 3–4 minutes or until piping hot. Season, then serve immediately. **Total cooking time 20 minutes.**

spicy szechuan tofu

Serves **4**
Total cooking time **20 minutes**

4 tablespoons **vegetable oil**
6 **spring onions**, finely sliced
2 **red chillies**, deseeded and
  thinly sliced
2.5 cm (1 in) piece of **fresh
  root ginger**, finely chopped
4 **garlic cloves**, finely sliced
1 teaspoon crushed **Szechuan
  peppercorns**
pinch of **salt**
250 g (8 oz) **firm tofu**, cut into
  2.5 cm (1 in) cubes
200 g (7 oz) **mangetout**,
  halved
150 g (5 oz) **baby sweetcorn**,
  halved lengthways
250 g (8 oz) **pak choi**,
  chopped
300 g (10 oz) **beansprouts**
2 tablespoons **light soy sauce**
2 tablespoons **Shaohsing
  rice wine**
sesame oil, for drizzling
steamed **rice**, to serve

Heat 2 tablespoons of the oil in a wok or deep frying pan and add the spring onions, chillies, ginger, garlic, peppercorns and a pinch of salt. Fry for 1 minute, add the tofu and stir-fry for another 2 minutes, then transfer to a plate.

Add the remaining oil to the wok or pan and stir-fry the mangetout, sweetcorn, pak choi and beansprouts for a few minutes, until starting to wilt, then add the soy sauce and rice wine.

Return the tofu mixture to the wok or pan and toss everything together.

Drizzle with sesame oil and serve with rice.

For speedy Szechuan stir-fry, cube 500 g (1 lb) firm tofu and grill under a preheated medium grill for 2–3 minutes until golden brown. Meanwhile, heat 2 tablespoons vegetable oil in a wok or deep frying pan. Add 2 x 300 g (10 oz) packs stir-fry vegetables and stir-fry for 3–4 minutes. Stir in a 150 g (5 oz) sachet ready-made Szechuan stir-fry sauce and stir-fry for a further 1–2 minutes. Add the tofu to the pan, toss to mix and serve. **Total cooking time 10 minutes.**

puffed goats' cheese omelette

Serves **4**
Total cooking time **20 minutes**

6 eggs
25 g (1 oz) grated **Parmesan cheese**
handful of chopped **basil**
1 tablespoon **olive oil**
3 **roasted red peppers**, from a jar, drained and sliced
125 g (4 oz) **soft goats' cheese**
salt and **pepper**

Crack 3 eggs into a bowl. Separate the remaining 3 eggs and add the yolks to the whole eggs. Stir in the Parmesan and some of the basil and season to taste.

Whisk the egg whites until soft peaks form, then carefully fold into the whole egg mixture, one-third at a time.

Heat the oil in an ovenproof frying pan. Add the egg mixture and cook for 2 minutes, then scatter over the peppers and goats' cheese.

Place the pan under a preheated hot grill and cook for 5–7 minutes more until puffed and just set. Scatter over the remaining basil to serve.

For pecorino & chilli omelettes, heat 1 tablespoon butter in a small frying pan. Pour in 1 lightly beaten egg and stir around the pan. Leave to cook for 30 seconds until starting to set, then grate over 25 g (1 oz) pecorino cheese and add a pinch of dried red chilli flakes. Cook until the omelette is set, then roll it up and keep warm. Make 3 more omelettes in the same way. Serve with a green salad. **Total cooking time 10 minutes.**

spiced carrot & green bean stew

Serves **4**

Total cooking time **30 minutes**

1 tablespoon **sunflower oil**

1 **onion**, sliced

1–2 **hot green chillies**,
 deseeded and sliced

1 **garlic clove**, crushed

5–6 **fresh curry leaves**

1 tablespoon **medium curry
 powder**

¼ teaspoon **ground turmeric**

½ teaspoon **fenugreek seeds**

2 **carrots**, peeled and cut into
 thin matchsticks

450 g (14½ oz) **green beans,**
 trimmed and halved

400 ml (14 fl oz) **coconut milk**

juice of 1 **lime**

salt and **pepper**

steamed **rice** or **crusty bread**,
 to serve (optional)

Heat the oil in a heavy-based saucepan, add the onion, chillies, garlic and curry leaves and cook over a medium heat, stirring occasionally, for 6–8 minutes until the onion is softened and golden brown. Sprinkle over the curry powder, turmeric and fenugreek seeds and season well.

Add the carrots and beans and cook, stirring, for a further 3–4 minutes. Reduce the heat to low, pour over the coconut milk and simmer for 10–12 minutes or until the vegetables are tender.

Remove from the heat and stir in the lime juice. Ladle into bowls and serve with steamed rice or bread, if liked.

For spicy carrot & green bean soup, heat 1 tablespoon butter and 1 tablespoon sunflower oil in a heavy-based saucepan, add 1 finely chopped onion, 1 chopped garlic clove, 1 teaspoon peeled and grated fresh root ginger and 1 tablespoon mild curry powder and fry, stirring, for 1–2 minutes. Stir in 3 peeled and finely chopped carrots, 200 g (7 oz) finely chopped trimmed green beans and 800 ml (1 pint 8 fl oz) hot vegetable stock and bring to the boil, then reduce the heat to medium and cook for 12–15 minutes or until the vegetables are tender. Remove from the heat and, using a stick blender, process the soup until smooth. Season, then stir in 200 ml (7 fl oz) single cream. Serve with crusty bread. **Total cooking time 20 minutes.**

chunky vegetable red lentil dahl

Serves **4**
Total cooking time **30 minutes**

4 tablespoons **vegetable oil**
1 large **onion**, roughly
    chopped
1 **aubergine**, trimmed and
    roughly chopped
1 **red pepper**, cored,
    deseeded and cut into
    chunks
250 g (8 oz) **okra**, trimmed
    and cut into 2.5 cm (1 inch)
    lengths
175 g (6 oz) **split red lentils**,
    rinsed
3 tablespoons **balti curry
    paste**
600 ml (1 pint) **vegetable
    stock**
3 tablespoons chopped **mint**
200 g (7 oz) **natural yogurt**
5 tablespoons chopped **fresh
    coriander**
salt and **pepper**
warm **naan breads**, to serve

Heat the oil in a large, heavy-based saucepan and cook the onion and aubergine over a medium heat, stirring occasionally, for 5 minutes, until softened and cooked through.

Add the red pepper and okra to the pan and cook, stirring frequently, for 3–4 minutes before adding the lentils and curry paste. Stir well to mix, then pour in the stock. Bring to the boil, then reduce the heat, cover and simmer for 20 minutes until the lentils are tender.

Meanwhile, stir the mint into the yogurt.

Remove the pan from the heat, stir in the coriander and season to taste. Serve with warm naan breads and the minted yogurt for drizzling.

For quick red lentil, chunky vegetable & chilli soup, heat 2 tablespoons olive oil in a saucepan and cook 2 chopped onions, 1 deseeded and finely chopped red chilli, the finely grated rind of 1 lemon and 1 teaspoon ground cumin over a medium heat, stirring, for 2 minutes. Add 200 g (7 oz) rinsed split red lentils, 200 g (7 oz) frozen chunky mixed vegetables and 750 ml (1¼ pints) hot vegetable stock. Simmer for 8 minutes until the lentils are tender. Stir through shredded mint and serve with natural yogurt and pitta breads. **Total cooking time 10 minutes.**

cauliflower & potato curry

Serves **4**

Total cooking time **30 minutes**

3 tablespoons **vegetable oil**

1 large **onion**, roughly
  chopped

1 **cauliflower**, trimmed and cut
  into florets

500 g (1 lb) **potatoes**, peeled
  and cut into chunks

2 teaspoons **cumin seeds**

4 tablespoons **korma curry
  paste**

400 ml (14 fl oz) **coconut milk**

300 ml (½ pint) **vegetable
  stock**

300 g (10 oz) **spinach leaves**

4 tablespoons chopped **fresh
  coriander**

salt and **pepper**

warm **naan breads**, to serve

Heat the oil in a large, heavy-based saucepan and cook the onion over a medium heat, stirring occasionally, for 2–3 minutes until beginning to soften, then add the cauliflower, potatoes and cumin seeds. Cook for 4–5 minutes, stirring occasionally, until the potatoes are beginning to brown.

Add the curry paste and toss to coat the vegetables, then stir in the coconut milk and stock and bring to the boil. Reduce the heat, cover and simmer, stirring occasionally, for 20 minutes until the vegetables are tender, adding the spinach for the last 5 minutes of the cooking time.

Season generously and stir in the coriander. Serve with warm naan breads.

For cauliflower Thai green curry, cook a 500 g (1 lb) mixture of frozen cauliflower florets and green beans in a large saucepan of slightly salted boiling water according to the packet instructions. Drain and return to the pan. Add a 400 g (13 oz) jar Thai green curry sauce and heat through, stirring gently. Serve with ready-cooked Thai jasmine rice. **Total cooking time 10 minutes.**

malaysian red pepper & cabbage

Serves **4**
Total cooking time **20 minutes**

1 tablespoon **sunflower oil**
2 **garlic cloves**, crushed
2 teaspoons **medium curry
   powder**
1 **red pepper**, cored,
   deseeded and finely diced
½ **green cabbage**, finely
   shredded
3 **eggs**, lightly beaten
salt and **pepper**
crusty bread, to serve
   (optional)

Heat the oil in a large wok or frying pan until hot, add the garlic, curry powder and red pepper and stir-fry over a medium-high heat for 3–4 minutes until softened.

Increase the heat to high, add the cabbage, season and stir-fry for 5 minutes or until the cabbage is cooked but still retains a bite.

Stir in the eggs and mix well with the vegetables, then continue stirring until the eggs are scrambled and just cooked through. Serve immediately with crusty bread, if liked.

For spicy cabbage & red pepper stew, heat 2 tablespoons sunflower oil in a large saucepan, add 2 finely sliced onions and cook over a medium heat, stirring occasionally, for 6–8 minutes or until soft and translucent. Stir in 3 chopped garlic cloves, 1 deseeded and sliced red chilli and 1 tablespoon mild curry paste, then pour over 400 ml (14 fl oz) hot vegetable stock and 400 ml (14 fl oz) coconut milk and bring to the boil. Stir in ½ green cabbage, shredded, and 3 cored, deseeded and thinly sliced red peppers and bring back to the boil, then reduce the heat to medium and cook for 12–15 minutes or until the vegetables are tender. Season well, then serve with rice or crusty bread. **Total cooking time 30 minutes.**

mushroom & tofu stew

Serves **4**
Total cooking time **20 minutes**

1 tablespoon **olive oil**
1 **onion**, sliced
500 g (1 lb) **chestnut mushrooms**, quartered
350 g (11½ oz) **sweet potatoes**, peeled and chopped
½ tablespoon **pomegranate molasses** or **balsamic syrup**
1 tablespoon **wholemeal flour**
500 ml (17 fl oz) hot **vegetable stock**
1 tablespoon **dark muscovado sugar**
dash of **Worcestershire sauce**
200 g (7 oz) **tofu**, cubed
steamed **Tenderstem broccoli**, to serve

Heat the oil in a large saucepan or flameproof casserole dish, add the onion and cook for 1–2 minutes until it starts to soften. Add the mushrooms and cook for a further 1–2 minutes, stirring occasionally.

Add the sweet potatoes, molasses or syrup and flour and stir well. Slowly pour in the stock, stirring continuously. Add the sugar and Worcestershire sauce and stir again until well mixed.

Bring to a simmer, cover and cook for 15 minutes until the sweet potatoes are tender. Add the tofu 5 minutes before the end of the cooking time.

Serve with steamed Tenderstem broccoli.

For mushroom & tofu stir-fry, heat 1 tablespoon coconut oil in a wok or large frying pan, add 2 sliced red onions, 1 tablespoon mustard seeds and 2 chopped garlic cloves and stir-fry for 1–2 minutes. Add 500 g (1 lb) sliced chestnut mushrooms and stir-fry for 2–3 minutes, then add 1 cored, deseeded and sliced red pepper, ½ shredded Chinese cabbage and 150 g (5 oz) cubed tofu and stir-fry for a further 4–5 minutes. Stir in 2 teaspoons soy sauce. Serve sprinkled with 2 tablespoons toasted sesame seeds. **Total cooking time 10 minutes.**

jamaican spiced corn chowder

Serves **4**
Total cooking time **30 minutes**

1 tablespoon **olive oil**
1 large **onion**, finely chopped
2 **garlic cloves**, finely chopped
1 teaspoon **cayenne pepper**
200 g (7 oz) **red split lentils**, rinsed
1 litre (1¾ pints) hot **vegetable stock**
400 ml (14 fl oz) **coconut milk**
1 **Scotch bonnet chilli**, left whole
1 tablespoon **thyme leaves**
200 g (7 oz) **potatoes**, peeled and cut into 1 cm (½ in) dice
200 g (7 oz) **carrots**, peeled and cut into 1 cm (½ in) dice
400 g (13 oz) **sweetcorn kernels** (either fresh, frozen or canned)
2 **red peppers**, cored, deseeded and cut into 1 cm (½ in) dice
salt and **pepper**
handful of chopped **fresh coriander**, to garnish

Heat the oil in a saucepan and stir-fry the onion and garlic for 2–3 minutes.

Increase the heat, add the cayenne pepper, red lentils, stock, coconut milk, chilli, thyme, potatoes and carrots. Bring to the boil and simmer for 15–20 minutes.

Season and add the corn and red pepper for the last 3 minutes of cooking.

Remove the Scotch bonnet chilli, ladle the chowder into bowls and serve garnished with chopped coriander and sprinkled with freshly ground black pepper.

For corn & red pepper curry, heat 1 tablespoon olive oil in a saucepan and fry 1 chopped onion and 2 chopped garlic cloves with 625 g (1¼ lb) sweetcorn kernels and 2 cored, deseeded and finely diced red peppers for 1–2 minutes. Add 1 tablespoon mild curry powder and 600 ml (1 pint) coconut milk and bring to the boil. Cook for 3–4 minutes, remove from the heat and stir in 4 tablespoons finely chopped fresh coriander before serving over ready-cooked rice. **Total cooking time 10 minutes.**

desserts

vanilla zabaglione

Serves **4**
Total cooking time **10 minutes**

6 **egg yolks**
50 g (2 oz) **caster sugar**
1 **vanilla pod**
4 tablespoons **marsala** or
   dessert wine
biscotti, to serve

Place the egg yolks and sugar in a heatproof bowl. Split the vanilla pod lengthways, scrape out the seeds, add to the bowl and whisk together. Place the bowl over a saucepan of gently simmering water, taking care that the bottom of the bowl does not touch the water.

Add the marsala and whisk continuously with a hand-held electric whisk for 5–8 minutes until the mixture is frothy and thickened. It should leave a trail when you remove the beaters. Pour into glass serving bowls and serve with biscotti.

For vanilla egg nog, bring 500 ml (17 fl oz) milk and 200 ml (7 fl oz) single cream to the boil in a heavy-based saucepan with 1 split vanilla pod. Beat 4 egg yolks with 75 g (3 oz) caster sugar in a heatproof bowl to combine, then slowly pour on the hot milk, stirring continuously. Return to the pan and cook over a low heat for 5–10 minutes until thickened. Place 125 g (4 oz) chopped white chocolate in the heatproof bowl with 2 tablespoons brandy, if liked. Pour over the warm, thickened milk and stir until combined and the chocolate melted. Spoon into cups to serve. **Total cooking time 20 minutes.**

tropical fruit salad

Serves **4**

Total cooking time **20 minutes**

2 **lemon grass stalks**, roughly chopped

150 ml (¼ pint) **water**

150 g (5 oz) **caster sugar**

125 g (4 oz) **pineapple**, peeled and sliced

1 **mango**, peeled and sliced

½ **papaya**, peeled and chopped

coconut macaroons or **coconut ice cream**, to serve

Place the lemon grass, measurement water and sugar in a small, heavy-based saucepan, bring to the boil and cook for 1 minute. Let cool slightly, then transfer to the freezer until completely cool, about 10 minutes.

Arrange the fruit in a serving bowl. Strain the syrup over the fruit and serve with macaroons or coconut ice cream, if liked.

For sticky coconut rice with tropical fruit, cook 200 g (7 oz) pudding rice in a large saucepan of boiling water according to the pack instructions. Transfer to a colander to drain. Add 100 g (3½ oz) coconut cream, 3 tablespoons caster sugar and 1 lemon grass stalk to the pan and heat through. Return the rice to the pan, stir well and set aside for 10 minutes to cool. Peel and cut 1 mango and ½ pineapple into thin slices and serve with the coconut rice, topped with a sprinkling of desiccated coconut. **Total cooking time 30 minutes.**

rhubarb & ginger slump

Serves **4–6**

Total cooking time **30 minutes**

750 g (1 ½ lb) **rhubarb**,
trimmed and cut into chunks

1 tablespoon **self-raising
flour**

50 g (2 oz) **granulated sugar**

2 pieces of **stem ginger in
syrup**, drained and chopped,
plus 2 tablespoons **syrup
from the jar**

Topping

100 g (3½ oz) **self-raising
flour**

75 g (3 oz) **butter**, softened

75 g (3 oz) **granulated sugar**

4 tablespoons **milk**

1 **egg**, beaten

Place the rhubarb, flour, sugar, chopped ginger and syrup in a shallow ovenproof dish and toss together. Cover with foil and place in a preheated oven, 190°C (375°F), Gas Mark 5, for 3 minutes.

Meanwhile, place the ingredients for the topping in a food processor and blend until smooth. Uncover the rhubarb and spoon over the topping.

Return to the oven for a further 25 minutes or until the topping is golden and cooked through.

For rhubarb & ginger fools, whisk 200 ml (7 fl oz) double cream until soft peaks form, then stir in 1 tablespoon icing sugar. Gently stir in 125 g (4 oz) canned rhubarb, drained and chopped, and divide between serving bowls. Crumble 1 ginger biscuit over each portion and serve immediately. **Total cooking time 10 minutes.**

chocolate fondue

Serves **4**

Total cooking time **10 minutes**

300 ml (½ pint) **double cream**
2 tablespoons **orange liqueur**
  (optional)
150 g (5 oz) **dark chocolate**,
  chopped
150 g (5 oz) **milk chocolate**,
  chopped

To serve
marshmallows
biscuits
mini doughnuts

Bring the cream to the boil in a small, heavy-based saucepan. Remove from the heat and stir in the liqueur, if using, and the chocolate until melted. Transfer to a warmed serving bowl or fondue pot, if liked.

Arrange the marshmallows, biscuits and mini doughnuts on a serving plate, spear them on long forks and dip them into the warm chocolate.

For chocolate & marshmallow trifle, place 150 g (5 oz) mini marshmallows, 50 g (2 oz) butter and 250 g (8 oz) chopped chocolate in a heavy-based saucepan and melt over a low heat until smooth. Stand the pan in a bowl of cold water and leave to cool for 5–10 minutes. Whisk 250 ml (8 fl oz) double cream until it holds its shape, then stir in 1 teaspoon vanilla extract and the cooled chocolate mixture. Arrange bite-sized chunks of plain cake in the bottom of a serving dish and spoon the chocolate mixture on top. Scatter over a handful of raspberries and blueberries to serve. **Total cooking time 20 minutes.**

apple & orange tart

Serves **4**
Total cooking time **30 minutes**

300 g (10 oz) **ready-rolled
 puff pastry**
5 **apples**, such as Coxes,
 cored and thinly sliced
6 tablespoons **caster sugar**
finely grated rind of **1 orange**

Place the pastry on a baking sheet and use a sharp
knife to lightly score a 1 cm (½ inch) border round the
edges, taking care not to cut right through the pastry.
Prick all over the centre of the pastry with a fork.

Toss the apples with 5 tablespoons of the sugar and
the orange rind, then arrange on top of the pastry.
Sprinkle over the remaining sugar. Place in a preheated
oven, 220°C (425°F), Gas Mark 7, for 20 minutes until
the apples are tender and the pastry is crisp.

For apple & orange brioche tarts, cut out a round
from each of 4 slices of brioche, using a cup as a guide.
Butter both sides and arrange on a baking sheet. Mix
25 g (1 oz) ground almonds and 4 tablespoons caster
sugar with 3 tablespoons mascarpone cheese and
the finely grated rind of ½ orange, then spoon on to
the brioche. Arrange 2 cored and thinly sliced apples
on top, then sprinkle over 2 tablespoons caster sugar.
Place in a preheated oven, 200°C (400°F), Gas Mark 6,
for 15–20 minutes until golden. **Total cooking time
20 minutes.**

strawberry cream puffs

Serves **4**

Total cooking time **20 minutes**

300 g (10 oz) **ready-rolled puff pastry**
4 tablespoons **icing sugar**
300 ml (½ pint) **double cream**
300 g (10 oz) **strawberries**, hulled and halved

Cut the pastry into 12 equal rectangles and arrange on a baking sheet. Place another baking sheet on top to prevent the pastry from puffing up too much during cooking. Place in a preheated oven, 200°C (400°F), Gas Mark 6, for 10 minutes until golden and crisp.

Sift half the icing sugar over the pastry puffs and cook under a preheated hot grill for 30 seconds until the sugar melts. Leave to cool.

Whisk the cream with the remaining icing sugar until soft peaks form. Arrange the pastry strips, whipped cream and strawberries on plates and serve immediately.

For strawberry cream pots, whisk 300 ml (½ pint) double cream with ½ teaspoon vanilla extract and 2 tablespoons icing sugar until soft peaks form. Stir in 200 g (7 oz) hulled and chopped strawberries and divide between small glass bowls. Serve with shortbread biscuits. **Total cooking time 10 minutes.**

apricot & almond crostata

Serves **6–8**

Total cooking time **30 minutes**

butter, for greasing
icing sugar, for dusting
250 g (8 oz) **shortcrust pastry**
150 g (5 oz) **marzipan**, sliced
8 **apricots**, halved and stoned
25 g (1 oz) **flaked almonds**
2 tablespoons **milk**
2 tablespoons **caster sugar**

Lightly grease a baking sheet. Dust a work surface with icing sugar, then roll out the pastry into a 35 cm (14 inch) round. Place on the baking sheet, arrange the marzipan slices in the middle and top with the halved apricots.

Scatter the almonds over the top, then fold the edges of the pastry up and over to form a rough border. Brush the pastry border with the milk and sprinkle with the caster sugar.

Place in a preheated oven, 200°C (400°F), Gas Mark 6, for 25 minutes until the pastry is just cooked through. Serve with cream or custard, if liked.

For baked apricots stuffed with almonds, place 125 g (4 oz) amaretti biscuits in a food processor with 25 g (1 oz) blanched almonds, 1 egg white and 2 tablespoons sugar and pulse to form a rough paste. Halve 9 apricots, and arrange cut sides up in a shallow ovenproof dish, then place a little of the almond mixture on top of each apricot. Place in a preheated oven, 200°C (400°F), Gas Mark 6, for 10–15 minutes until the fruit is tender and the topping is crisp. **Total cooking time 20 minutes.**

cinnamon-spiced cherries

Serves **4**
Total cooking time **10 minutes**

25 g (1 oz) **caster sugar**
350 ml (12 fl oz) **rosé wine**
strip of pared **lemon** rind
1 **cinnamon stick**
500 g (1 lb) **cherries**, pitted

Combine all the ingredients in a saucepan. Bring to the boil, then reduce the heat and simmer for 5 minutes until the sugar has dissolved and the cherries are tender.

Use a slotted spoon to transfer the cherries to a serving dish, then cook the liquid over a high heat for 3–4 minutes until syrupy. Remove the cinnamon and lemon rind, then pour over the cherries and serve warm or cold.

For cherry & cinnamon soup, heat 450 ml (¾ pint) fruity white wine in a saucepan with 75 g (3 oz) caster sugar, 1 cinnamon stick, 1 strip of pared orange rind and a good squeeze of orange juice. Simmer for 10 minutes, then add 500 g (1 lb) pitted cherries and cook for 5 minutes until tender. Remove the orange rind and cinnamon, add 150 ml (¼ pint) mascarpone cheese and purée with a stick blender until smooth. Add a few ice cubes to cool the soup, then spoon into serving bowls and scatter with chocolate shavings and a few more pitted cherries. **Total cooking time 20 minutes.**

chocolate fudge brownie

Serves **8**
Total cooking time **30 minutes**

200 g (7 oz) **butter**
200 g (7 oz) **dark chocolate**,
  chopped
175 g (6 oz) **soft dark brown
  sugar**
150 g (5 oz) **caster sugar**
4 **eggs**, beaten
50 g (2 oz) **ground almonds**
75 g (3 oz) **plain flour**
vanilla ice cream, to serve
  (optional)

Melt the butter and chocolate over a low heat in a
shallow ovenproof dish, about 23 cm (9 inches) across.
Remove from the heat and cool for a couple of minutes.

Beat together the sugars and eggs, then stir in the
chocolate mixture followed by the almonds and flour.

Wipe the rim of the ovenproof dish with a damp piece
of kitchen paper to neaten, then pour in the mixture.
Place in a preheated oven, 180°C (350°F), Gas Mark 4,
for 25 minutes until just set.

Serve warm with vanilla ice cream, if liked.

For malted brownie sundaes, bring 150 ml (¼ pint)
double cream to the boil in a small, heavy-based
saucepan. Remove from the heat and stir in 100 g
(3½ oz) chopped dark chocolate until smooth. Cut
200 g (7 oz) ready-made brownies into small squares
and place in the bottom of sundae glasses. Add
2 scoops of vanilla ice cream to each glass, then
drizzle over the chocolate sauce. Roughly crush 50 g
(2 oz) malted chocolate sweets and scatter over the
top to serve. **Total cooking time 10 minutes.**

syrup sponge pudding

Serves **6**
Total cooking time **20 minutes**

175 g (6 oz) **butter**, softened,
  plus extra for greasing
175 g (6 oz) **caster sugar**
175 g (6 oz) **self-raising flour**
1 teaspoon **baking powder**
3 **eggs**
1 teaspoon **vanilla extract**
3 tablespoons **milk**
finely grated rind of ½ **lemon**
6 tablespoons **golden syrup**
cream or **custard**, to serve

Grease a 1.2 litre (2 pint) pudding basin. Place all the ingredients, except the golden syrup, in a food processor and blend until smooth. Spoon 4 tablespoons of the golden syrup into the bottom of the basin, then add the pudding mixture and smooth the surface with a knife.

Cover with microwave-proof clingfilm and pierce the film a couple of times with a sharp knife. Cook in a microwave oven on medium heat for about 12 minutes. Test to see if it is cooked by inserting a skewer into the pudding; it should come out clean.

Leave to rest for 3 minutes, then turn out on to a deep plate and spoon over the remaining golden syrup. Serve with cream or custard.

For syrup-topped hotcakes, place 200 g (7 oz) self-raising flour in a food processor with 1 teaspoon baking powder, 2 eggs, 250 ml (8 fl oz) milk and a pinch of salt and blend until smooth. Heat a large, nonstick frying pan. Add a little butter and swirl around the pan, then add generous tablespoonfuls of the batter. Cook for 2 minutes until starting to set, then turn over and cook for a further 1 minute. Remove from the pan, keep warm and repeat with the remaining batter. Serve the cakes scattered with blueberries and drizzled generously with golden syrup. **Total cooking time 10 minutes.**

lemon syllabub

Serves **4**
Total cooking time **10 minutes**

300 ml (½ pint) **double cream**
75 ml (3 fl oz) **sweet white wine**
50 g (2 oz) **caster sugar**
finely grated rind and juice of ½ **lemon**

Whisk the cream until it just starts to hold its shape. Add the wine, one-third at a time, whisking well between each addition.

Stir in the sugar and lemon juice and continue whisking until fluffy and thick. Spoon into glasses, scatter with lemon rind and serve.

For little lemon puddings, beat 50 g (2 oz) butter and 75 g (3 oz) caster sugar with the finely grated rind of 1 lemon until light and fluffy. Add 2 egg yolks and 4 tablespoons lemon juice. Stir in 1 tablespoon flour, then 100 ml (3½ fl oz) double cream and 150 ml (¼ pint) milk until smooth. Pour into 4 lightly greased 200 ml (7 fl oz) ramekins. Place the ramekins in a shallow roasting tin and pour boiling water into the tin until it comes halfway up the ramekins. Place in a preheated oven, 180°C (350°F), Gas Mark 4, for 20–25 minutes until golden and slightly risen. **Total cooking time 30 minutes.**

prune clafoutis

Serves **4**
Total cooking time **30 minutes**

butter, for greasing
3 **eggs**
125 g (4 oz) **caster sugar**
50 g (2 oz) **plain flour**
150 ml (¼ pint) **double cream**
150 ml (¼ pint) **milk**
1 teaspoon **vanilla extract**
75 g (3 oz) **pitted soft prunes**

Lightly grease a shallow ovenproof dish. Whisk together the eggs and sugar until pale, frothy and tripled in volume. Sift the flour into the bowl and lightly fold in. Add the cream, milk and vanilla extract and mix until just combined.

Pour into the ovenproof dish and place in a preheated oven, 190°C (375°F), Gas Mark 5, for 5 minutes until the surface is just starting to set. Scatter over the prunes, then return to the oven for a further 15–20 minutes until the clafoutis is risen and golden.

For plum crisp, halve and stone 200 g (7 oz) plums and place in a lightly greased ovenproof dish. Cut 25 g (1 oz) butter into small pieces and scatter over the plums with 2 tablespoons caster sugar. Cover with foil and place in a preheated oven, 200°C (400°F), Gas Mark 6, for 10 minutes. Meanwhile, crush 125 g (4 oz) ginger biscuits and mix with 25 g (1 oz) softened butter. Remove the foil and scatter the biscuit mixture over the plums. Return to the oven for a further 5 minutes until lightly crisp. **Total cooking time 20 minutes.**

crunchy berry brûlée

Serves **4**

Total cooking time **20 minutes**

250 g (8 oz) **mascarpone cheese**

300 ml (½ pint) **ready-made fresh custard**

150 g (5 oz) **mixed berries**

100 g (3½ oz) **caster sugar**

1 ½ tablespoons **water**

Beat the mascarpone until smooth, then gently stir in the custard and transfer the mixture to a serving dish. Scatter the berries on top.

Place the sugar and measurement water in a small, heavy-based saucepan and slowly bring to the boil, carefully swirling the pan from time to time. Keep cooking until the sugar dissolves, then turns a deep caramel colour. Pour over the berries and leave for a few minutes to harden.

For melting berry yogurt, place 200 g (7 oz) mixed berries in a serving dish. Spoon over 300 ml (½ pint) natural yogurt, then sprinkle with 75 g (3 oz) soft dark brown sugar. Chill in the refrigerator for 20–25 minutes until the sugar has melted. **Total cooking time 30 minutes.**

passion fruit & mango mess

Serves **4**
Total cooking time **10 minutes**

300 ml (½ pint) **double cream**
2–3 tablespoons **icing sugar**
4 **meringue nests**, crushed
1 **mango**, peeled and sliced
1 **passion fruit**, halved

Whisk the cream with the icing sugar until it just holds its shape.

Gently stir in the meringue, most of the mango and a little of the passion fruit pulp.

Spoon into glasses and top with the remaining fruit.

For passion fruit & mango cream, peel and chop 1 mango and divide between 4 glasses. Whisk 1 egg yolk with 2 tablespoons caster sugar until very frothy and pale, then stir in the pulp of 2 passion fruit. Whisk 200 ml (7 fl oz) double cream until soft peaks form, then stir into the egg mixture and whisk until thickened. Add 1 tablespoon orange liqueur and 75 g (3 oz) crushed meringues. Spoon over the mango and top with a little more chopped fruit, if liked. **Total cooking time 20 minutes.**

index

239

acknowledgements

Commissioning editor: Eleanor Maxfield
Editor: Polly Poulter
Designer: Tracy Killick
Production controller: Allison Gonsalves

Photography: Octopus Publishing Group Limited: Stephen
Conroy 7 right, 63, 75, 100-101, 105, 119, 137, 152-153,
161, 185, 195, 197, 204-205; Will Heap 6, 7 left, 8, 9 right,
19, 27, 41, 65, 67, 77, 79, 87, 95, 97, 111, 117, 123, 125,
127, 129, 131, 135, 149, 151, 155, 159, 163, 165, 171,
175, 179, 181, 187, 189, 191, 193, 199, 203; David Munns
10-11; Lis Parsons 1, 13, 17, 23, 29, 31, 33, 39, 43, 45, 47,
49, 59, 60-61, 69, 83, 93, 133, 139, 143, 145, 147, 167,
177, 183, 201; William Shaw 2, 4, 9 left, 15, 21, 25, 35, 37,
51, 53, 55, 57, 71, 73, 81, 85, 89, 91, 99, 103, 107, 109, 113,
115, 121, 141, 157, 169, 173, 207, 209, 211, 213, 215, 217,
219, 221, 223, 225, 227, 229, 231, 233.